Uncommon Heroes

A CELEBRATION OF HEROES AND ROLE MODELS FOR GAY AND LESBIAN AMERICANS

EXECUTIVE EDITOR
Phillip Sherman

EDITED BY
Samuel Bernstein

27 December 1994

Michael —

I'm really glad we met through U.N.'s. I'm looking forward to getting to know you better. Best Wishes for '95.

FLETCHER PRESS NEW YORK

Executive Editor
Phillip Sherman

Editor
Samuel Bernstein

Editorial Advisor
David Groff

Editorial Consultants
John R. Selig
Geoffrey Staples

Graphic Designer
Arch Garland, Flyleaf

Graphic Consultant/Cover Design
David Fletcher

Operations Manager
F.J. Lopez-Baez

Copy Editor
Richard Eric Weigle

*I dedicate this
book to my father
and to Paco.
Without their
influence
and support,*
Uncommon
Heroes *could
never have
existed. Their
uncommon
courage to press
forward with
life despite its
complications
has inspired me
deeply.*

–Phillip Sherman

PREFACE

My son Morty was at the Stonewall Bar when the riots began. Most of the people there were used to being harassed and mistreated by the police. But something snapped that night. A small group of gay men and lesbians decided to stand up for themselves and rebel. Soon the group grew larger, and larger still. They courageously kept the police at bay with bricks, bottles, and anything else they could get their hands on. It was a dramatic turning point in the gay and lesbian civil rights movement. Although we didn't know it at the time, those days in June 1969 opened new horizons for my family. In the years that followed, standing proudly beside Morty enriched and changed my life.

The first time I marched with him in a parade, I carried a sign that said *Parents of Gays: Unite in Support for Our Children*. The response was just overwhelming. People cheered when they saw us. They came out of the crowd into the street and kissed me. And they asked me to talk to their parents. That's when I knew I had to form Parents and Friends of Lesbians and Gays (P-FLAG). It has given me the opportunity to know so many gay and lesbian heroes from all walks of life. I am still amazed, inspired, and sometimes moved to tears at their courage.

Uncommon Heroes tells the stories of over one hundred extraordinary men and women who are gay or lesbian: couples like Del Martin and Phyllis Lyon, who have been together for over forty years; philanthropists like James Hormel and James Pepper, who have used their financial resources to help build a lesbian and gay community; and people like Dr. Richard Pillard, the first psychiatrist in the United States to publicly come out to the closet. Read about the triumphs of Elton John, Martina Navratilova, and Olympic Gold Medalists Bruce Hayes and Greg Louganis; get to know how Paul Monette and Rita Mae Brown began writing; and learn what Virginia Apuzzo and Congressman Barney Frank think about gay and lesbian political power. But remember, while the people in this book are certainly heroes, they are just a few of the many who have set proud examples. For every Roberta Achtenberg or Harvey Fierstein, there are many others equally deserving of recognition.

This book is important for two reasons: gay and lesbian people desperately need to come face-to-face with gay and lesbian people who positively represent a diverse and proud community that is so poorly understood; and the rest of us need to eliminate our own ignorance and prejudice. *Uncommon Heroes* will make you laugh and it will make you cry. But I hope that you won't forget the work that still has to be done.

—Jeanne Manford, founder of P-FLAG

I have strong memories of hearing about gay people "fighting back" at a place called "Stonewall" in 1969. I didn't know where that was then—I was ten years old and I lived in Los Angeles—yet somehow I knew that it was important, that it had something to do with me. But what? Well, that was a secret; a whisper in the back of my mind. In the years that followed, as I became more and more certain of what that voice was saying, I still kept it hidden, because like so many kids, I was scared that if I told someone, it might make it that much more real. And I was afraid that people would hate me. But the pressure of living a lie became too much to bear.

My first step out of the closet was telling my family. We talked about it with a therapist, and they became my allies as I began to live free of fear and shame. But looking back, I've often thought how much easier it might have been for me and my family if we had known about a few gay or lesbian people of achievement. See, I didn't want to be gay because I thought it meant that I would never be able to accomplish the things I dreamed about: building a business, going into politics, or having a home one day with someone I love.

But I learned that lesbians and gay men can do anything, and later an idea began to slowly take shape, a way for new generations to know that their future possibilities are limitless. I am very grateful to Keith Meinhold and Roberta Achtenberg, for it was their national visibility that provided the final push, the catalyst, for what has become *Uncommon Heroes*—exactly the kind of book I wish I'd had when I was growing up—with stories about courageous people who happen to be gay or lesbian, who choose to live their lives outside the closet, and who challenge American society's beliefs about the lives we lead.

Over the course of two years, I talked with hundreds of lesbians and gay men across the country. I asked everyone I met to tell me who encouraged and inspired them. It was extremely difficult to narrow that list down to the group of heroes and role models here. In truth, there are hundreds, even thousands more, who are equally as special. Write to us. Let us know of other heroes you would like to see in future editions.

This was a labor of love. But when the fun was only a distant memory and the tough going got even tougher, a special team of uncommon heroes rose to that call: Paco Lopez-Baez, Samuel Bernstein, Arch Garland, Anita Merk, Donal Holway, David Morgan, John R. Selig, Michelle Karlsberg, Geoffrey Staples, Gail Ensinger, David Fletcher, Richard Eric Weigle, Jim Berry, Kimberly Stisi, Jerrald Boswell, Ron Anderegg, Skip Koons, Brenda Shaughnessy, Gaylord Hoftiezer, Stephen Frankel, Lli Wilburn, and Jerry Young. I thank them with all my heart.

—P. S.

Roberta Achtenberg

ATTORNEY AND FEDERAL OFFICIAL

As a lesbian and a Jew, I have had to live with the fear for my physical safety and that of my people. Leaders like George Bush have scapegoated people like me—and families like mine—by charging that we are destroying America. What is destroying America is lack of opportunity, the abandonment of justice, and the harangues of false prophets.

When civil rights attorney Roberta Achtenberg took the podium in front of San Francisco's City Hall for a press conference to discuss her nomination by President Bill Clinton to a post in his new government, she was making history. The outspoken and sharply articulate forty-three-year-old civil rights attorney, partner of Judge Mary Morgan, adoptive mother of Benjamin, and high profile activist, had been chosen to serve as Assistant Secretary for Fair Housing and Equal Opportunity in the federal government's Department of Housing and Urban Development. It was the highest level government position for which any President had nominated an openly gay or lesbian person.

Achtenberg's nomination was the culmination of decades of hard and selfless work. As an attorney, law professor, law school dean, and guiding force behind the San Francisco-based Lesbian Rights Project and its successor, the National Center for Lesbian Rights (NCLR), Achtenberg had worked for much of her adult life to secure equal rights for lesbian and gay people. Her subsequent election to the San Francisco Board of Supervisors brought her inside the governmental process, and set the stage for her selection by President Clinton.

During the years she served as executive director of NCLR, Achtenberg fought for the legal recognition of relationships between non-biological and non-adoptive lesbian and gay co-parents and their children. "I can't think of any other single thing I've done professionally that has given me more joy," she says. And given the presence of her son Benjamin, it was clearly a professional act with her supreme personal concern. In her new role in the federal government, Achtenberg has the opportunity to influence national housing policy, and to serve as a role model for gay and lesbian people who choose to be themselves. While she isn't all that comfortable with being called a role model, she says, "If young people get to view me as acting like the regular person I am, that's the kind of contribution I'm delighted to be able to make."

Senate confirmation of Roberta Achtenberg to the Department of Housing and Urban Development has sent a message that discrimination, wherever it occurs, is unacceptable, and that the promise of equal opportunity is alive and well in this great nation.

—Barbara Boxer
CALIFORNIA SENATOR

1

Keith Meinhold

SAILOR U.S. NAVY

I had actually fantasized about it before I was even asked. I thought about going on television to say how unfair the ban is. But once I did it, I knew that it would have to be all or nothing—I would have to do everything just right and be perfect, because if I didn't, I'd be failing so many people. I took that to heart, I really did—how whatever I said would affect the lives of so many in the gay and lesbian community. I just wanted to get it right.

Keith Meinhold, a young Navy flight instructor at California's Moffett Field, had been working with a group of gay veterans in early 1992, covertly helping gay and lesbian service personnel who were thrown out of the military. He liked the Navy, but the news trickling in on the grapevine was grim. He learned that, to cap off months of witch-hunts that had started in the Pacific, the Navy would discharge over fifty gay men and lesbians in the Bay Area within a matter of weeks. His small cadre of veterans providing help and counseling would never be able to meet the legal and financial needs of so many people at once.

Outrage propelled Meinhold into adding his voice to the growing chorus challenging the military ban. He called his parents and told them to be prepared: He was going to publicly discuss his homosexuality on ABC's *World News Tonight,* and put a human face on the issue. His earnest simplicity struck a chord with many viewers. But within months of his television appearance, and despite an exemplary record, Meinhold was discharged from the Navy.

"They just didn't understand what I was fighting for," Meinhold says. "It was much more than a job, it was honor and basic liberty. I just don't think the Navy got that at all." But the tall, lanky California native proved a scrappy, media-savvy combatant when he sued in federal court, contending that his discharge violated the Constitution's equal-protection guarantee. In a landmark decision in November 1992, a federal district judge ordered the Navy to reinstate him. Meinhold became the first member of the armed forces to return to active service following dismissal for homosexuality, and was welcomed back to Moffett Field by most of his colleagues. "The story is that there's really no story," he says. "I've been treated well since my return and given good assignments. Maybe *that's* the real story."

Meinhold has been in the Navy since age seventeen, and plans to remain in the service for another six or seven years. "I was very introverted as a child," he says, "but the Navy changed that. They told me that I was doing well, that I was at the top of my class and successful. After twelve years of hearing that kind of thing, it convinced me that maybe I could be a leader. In a way, the Navy must feel like they created a monster!"

Keith Meinhold represents for this generation of gays and lesbians, what Rosa Parks represented for African-Americans and what Cesar Chavez represented for Hispanic-Americans— an individual whose act of courage changed the world.

—David B. Mixner
POLITICAL CONSULTANT

Written by Sharon P. Holland

Audre Lorde

POET AND PHILOSOPHER

This is why work is important: Its power doesn't lie in the me that lives in the words as much as in the heart's blood pumping behind the eye that is reading, the muscle behind the desire that is sparked by the word—hope as a living state that propels us, open-eyed and fearful, into all the battles of our lives. And some of those battles we do not win. And some we do.

Audre Lorde was a Black woman. A lesbian. A feminist. A mother of two children. A daughter of Grenadian immigrants. An educator. An activist. She was arguably the most influential figure in the lesbian community, out in the late 1950s during a time when lesbian visibility, let alone *Black* lesbian visibility, was certainly not chic or common—and she was a role model to many who would come after her. But first and foremost, it is her work that endures. Lorde was a writer of astounding insight.

As both a lesbian poet-philosopher and a feminist critic, Lorde consistently reminded us to resist seeing one another through the lens of racism, sexism, and homophobia. She encouraged us to discover new ways of being in the world and with one another. Her work, life, and poetry rejected the very White, Western, and male notion that theory and praxis are two competing entities; she believed that our attempts to resolve the differences between one another ultimately lead to a sense of disconnectedness in our communities and our world. Her global vision was not one of homogeneity or plasticized diversity, but a sense of community that draws in the sheer strength of differences across lives—a recognition that can lead to revolutionary change and insight. Always willing to challenge the feminist manifest "the personal is political," Lorde made no secret of her life's pain and power—sharing with us her struggle with cancer and her wellspring of the erotic. Her essay *Uses of the Erotic as Power* is perhaps one of the most vital pieces of feminist criticism and philosophy written during the late twentieth century, removing the debate from the dichotomy between the erotic and the pornographic, and viewing instead the erotic as a site of power, knowledge, and creativity.

During a career that spanned five decades, Lorde's nine published books of poetry include *Black Unicorn, Coal,* and *Cables to Rage;* her five works of prose include *A Burst of Light, Sister Outsider,* and *Zami.* She died on November 17, 1992 after a fourteen-year struggle with cancer. Audre Lord has left us not only a voice, but a spirit that guides, and a body of works that continues to speak to our many and varied truths.

Audre Lorde's poetry summons us to our ancestral beauty. Terrible and sweet. Tough and soft. Ancient and modern. As she weaves a legacy of imagery, her words become constant awakenings, making us walk and talk a mouth of truths. A season change. A life of honor.

—Sonia Sanchez
POET

Scot Nakagawa

ACTIVIST

If my work does not stand for the rights of poor and working people, then I do not stand on the side of justice. I am of the poor, and I want more than anything to stand on the side of justice.

One evening in 1989 Scot Nakagawa was bicycling home from his job at Burnside Projects, a center for homeless and low-income people in Portland, Oregon. A carload of skinheads began accosting him— pursuing him for several blocks while shouting racist political slogans. Nakagawa escaped by riding into an alley and onto a construction site. He was well aware of how much danger he was in: a year earlier skinheads in Portland had beaten a Black Ethiopian man to death with baseball bats.

After his escape, Nakagawa decided to fight back. Already a seasoned grassroots activist at the time of the attack, he has spent the last five years specializing in countering right wing political groups. He is the former director of the Coalition for Human Dignity (a Northwest anti-Klan group), and co-founder of Portland's Homophobic Violence Documentation Project, as well as of the People of Faith Against Bigotry. Nakagawa was also a field organizer for Oregon's No on 9 campaign that helped defeat an anti-gay ballot measure in 1992. His ability to connect with different kinds of people and his faith in what groups can accomplish collectively, have made it possible for him to work effectively as an activist; organizing for decent housing, child care, and health services, as well as for gay and lesbian rights.

Nakagawa feels that he learned his most important lessons about organizing from his grandmother while growing up in Hawaii. She was a labor organizer who participated in some of America's most successful workers' struggles against the powerful corporations that owned the sugar plantations where she worked cutting cane most of her life. She taught Nakagawa the true power of community, how the best organizers are motivated by a spirit of humility and joy—and not a little courage.

Scot was among the first in the lesbian and gay community to identify the broad agenda of the right and to connect their members and groups in a way that makes sense. He has played an essential role in shaping and broadening our politics and our strategies.

—Suzanne Pharr
WOMEN'S PROJECT

Ian McKellen

ACTOR

I do think show business is a little different from other industries, and there are many lesbians and gays who are out and will be able to protect each other in some ways. It's really yet to be tested whether a young actor at the outset of his career could say he was gay and the force of his personality was such that directors and producers and television sponsors would be prepared to have him play a straight character.

Until very recently, few Americans were aware of the acclaimed English actor, Sir Ian McKellen, but over the last five years, his name and face have become familiar. Though theatre-goers saw him play Mozart's rival in Amadeus, and film fans noticed him in *Plenty,* it is only since his recent television appearances in *And The Band Played On* and *Tales of the City*—plus his very public coming out—that he has truly become a famous person in the United States. "Revealing my sexuality changed me as a person," he said. "It changed my self-confidence, and my attitude toward the world. It's released in me an anger and a passion to get laws changed in the United Kingdom. All that was bound to affect my acting, and now it seems commonplace amongst critics that I am a better actor than I used to be."

McKellen is able to utilize his talent and fame to do good for others: to help raise funds for AIDS organizations, to talk truthfully to the media about gay and lesbian issues, and to serve as a role model. His artistry and activism give him a unique perspective on America. "The distinction to make between the United Kingdom and the United States is that homophobia is not well-organized in the UK," he says. "It exists of course, it's institutionalized, it's there in the law of the land, but there are no equivalents to the Moral Majority or the fundamentalist churches."

It might have once been unimaginable for an actor of Sir Ian McKellen's stature to openly acknowledge his sexual orientation. Watching him flirt with Patrick Swayze on *The Tonight Show,* with Jay Leno taking it all in stride, makes one thing perfectly clear: those days are over. "It seems to me," says McKellen, "that out gay actors, far from being reviled by the world, are rather welcome."

Until he came out, McKellen was simply one of our greatest living actors, but it has been as a gay man that he has drawn perhaps his loudest kudos. His coming out, done as a protest against Britain's homophobic Section 29 law, not only increased his gossip-fodder quotient, but also set him on an unflagging activist path, where professing his human rights views goes hand in glove with expressing his artistry on-stage and on film.

–Michele Kort

THE ADVOCATE

Written by Denis Chicola ◊ Photographed by Marc Geller

Elton John

SINGER/SONGWRITER
I can't compromise my life anymore. I'm not going to.

Who would have guessed? Little Reggie Dwight dancing the charleston with Diana, Princess of Wales. Definitely a moment to make you believe in fairy tales. Just the two of them. In a ballroom. In Buckingham Palace. If only those kids who had taunted him throughout his childhood could see him—the bullies who had made him feel alone, even when he was among a sea of children, and his father, who had insisted Reggie only was getting what he deserved. *If they could see him now.* Reggie Dwight, alone, with the mythical woman the world can't get enough of.

Not too long ago, John was usually camouflaged—by extravagant costumes, a larger-than-life stage personality, and silence. But Reggie Dwight was always there, the boy inside the man, still terrified of being discovered—the universal battle fought by so many gay men and lesbians. Behind the glasses and the sequins, John would watch the world watch him. Did they know? Could they tell? Did they care? He had spoken to the press in the seventies about being "bisexual," yet he still felt a certain shame about being who he is; a shame he tried to numb through sex, drugs, rock and roll, and food. Until the morning he opened the *New York Times* and read about Ryan White.

Finally John's eyes were opened to a much larger world. For the first time, he saw his own problems diminish as he reached beyond himself, to join hands with Ryan White and his family in their battle against AIDS. The dark shadows that had hovered over John began to dissipate in the light of his concern for another person's struggle. And he wasn't just a fairy godfather, flying into the White family's lives in a blaze of money and publicity. He stayed with them. He helped them through the day-to-dayness of hospitals, of debilitating, painful medical treatments, and through the terrible fear that illness brings to a family. It's so easy for a celebrity to do a benefit or sing in a telethon. Elton John became part of Ryan White's life. And part of his death.

Now John has wrestled with his demons, and put away his masks. He is at last comfortable with himself, and is in a committed relationship. He has also become a leader—using his name, his music, his AIDS foundation, and his new-found ease with his sexuality to help forge a future free of AIDS and bigotry. It's been a roller coaster ride. But Ryan White spoke with the wisdom of children when he said, "Elton John isn't afraid to be different. Elton John is the best."

The more I've seen Elton John face himself, the more of a complete human being he has become. I think he wants to show people you can be up-front, and I think he's testing the barriers of society to see how far he can go.

—Bernie Taupin
LYRICIST

10

Nancy Lanoue

FOUNDER OF THE LESBIAN COMMUNITY CANCER CENTER

One in ten women will get breast cancer, yet we never know who has it; we don't see one another. I've never seen a woman in the gym who has had a mastectomy. Lesbians and other oppressed people have a bigger burden to bear because the rest of the world spends a lot of time telling us we should feel bad about ourselves. There's been a lot of damage that we have to undo.

When I watch Nancy Lanoue in action, or listen to her speak, it seems to me that her chief business in life is to encourage every woman who crosses her path to become more confident. We value her as we value few teachers in our lives.

—Karen Lee Osborne

As Jeanette Pappas lay dying in 1989 from pancreatic cancer, she insisted on planning her own funeral and asked her life partner, Nancy Lanoue, to speak at her service. She told Lanoue she didn't want her to down-play the issue of her cancer. Rather, she wanted Lanoue to tell the world that this was one lesbian who was mad as hell to be dying from cancer at the age of forty-seven. And Lanoue did tell.

At the time of Pappas' illness, Lanoue herself had already endured a bitter recovery from breast cancer. But her bitterness was not simply a side effect of the chemotherapy. Upon diagnosis, Lanoue had quickly discovered the dearth of support for women with cancer in the Chicago area, particularly for lesbians. What support there was often encouraged women to be ashamed of their supposed deformity which, it seemed, was supposed to be hidden as much as possible by prosthetic devices.

Lanoue was not an activist, and wasn't sure she wanted to become one, but encouraged by women with similar experiences, she helped start the Lesbian Community Cancer Project in 1990 and today serves as president of its board. The organization, modeled on AIDS organizations, now has a buddy program, support groups, free massage therapy, and a drop-in center and resource library. It is a living reminder of Lanoue's determination that no lesbian should face cancer alone.

Flexing her activist muscles in a different direction led Lanoue to teach martial arts, where instead of empowering women to fight illness, she helps them protect themselves from violence. Together, Lanoue and Sarah Ludden, her life partner since 1991, own and operate Thousand Waves, a martial arts school. Lanoue's interest in martial arts began when she took a self-defense course while a reporter for the *New York Post*. She later started SAFE, the Safety Fitness Exchange, New York City's first community-based organization centered on self-defense and rape prevention for women, and eventually earned a fourth-degree black belt.

In 1993, Nancy Lanoue's extraordinary courage and dedication were singled out, and she was elected to the Chicago Gay and Lesbian Hall of Fame.

Photographed by Tracy Baim
Courtesy Outlines Chicago

Marlon Riggs

DOCUMENTARY FILMMAKER

I know I'm not the obscenity that they would make of me. If nothing else, my struggle has allowed me to transcend that sense of shame and stigma identified with my being a Black gay man. Having come through that fire, they can't touch me.

Thirty-one and already successful as a documentary filmmaker, Marlon Riggs lay in a hospital bed in 1988, facing possible death from kidney failure and thinking about what he had—and had not—accomplished in his life. "I realized that I had become complicit in my own oppression," said Riggs, who had already drawn national attention for his 1987 film, *Ethnic Notions,* an Emmy award-winning documentary that examined the origins of the enduring and destructive stereotypes of African-Americans. "I could have gone the rest of my days dealing simply with race, extracting out sexuality. It would have made sense from a career perspective. But I thought, 'What am I doing with my life?' I knew there was a desperate need out there, from people who had never seen an affirming word or image about their lives. I thought, 'You have the capacity to do something about this, yet you are doing nothing.' "

That all changed when Riggs (recovered, but now aware he was HIV-positive) next made *Tongues Untied,* his bold documentary on Black gay men. Weaving poetry, rap, chanting, music and dance, *Tongues Untied* was also a chronicle of Riggs' own evolution, dramatizing not only his battles with racism and homophobia, but his long struggle toward self-acceptance as well. *Tongues Untied* met with both critical acclaim and vehement resistance. The *Chicago Tribune* called it "a powerful piece of filmmaking," and the *New York Times* declared it "a remarkable, rewarding effort," but the film was also at the center of more than one national political firestorm— parts of it were shown out of context on election-year television commercials sponsored by the religious right— and it was banned on several PBS affiliates.

Attempts to silence him made Riggs deeply angry. Realizing the importance of using that anger, he continued making films at an ever-increasing rate, finishing *Color Adjustment,* a sequel to *Ethnic Notions,* in 1991, along with a host of shorter pieces, including a 1993 documentary, *No Regrets,* which consisted of interviews with five Black gay men living with HIV. Riggs, who died in the Spring of 1994, saw a direct correlation between his own struggles and those of heroes from history like Harriet Tubman and Paul Robeson. "There's a parallel in terms of what I'm trying to do with my life," he said. "We're all motivated by our desire to affirm our worth as human beings."

To make a poetic, personal film in a culture that likes its documentaries matter-of-fact; that's a breakthrough.

—Tom Goldstein
U.C. BERKELEY

15

James Pepper

PHILANTHROPIST
I just help people get things done.

If gay life is a theatre performance, James Pepper is not exactly center stage—the lights would hurt his eyes and the applause would embarrass him. While other activists strut their stuff and, for better or worse, play to the crowd, Pepper works *back*stage, adjusting a costume, patting some nervous shoulders, lending the cash for that final set piece. But without Pepper and people like him, lesbian and gay society would be a sorry show indeed.

Pepper's manner resembles that of an extremely well-bred but mischievous schoolboy. Perfectly pressed, his trademark bowtie at a precise angle to the universe, he exhibits the droll and occasionally piercing charm of the Southern gentleman he is. But he is no stereotype. For generations, gay men like Pepper have stayed uptown, supporting correctly heterosexual charities, never venturing out of their well-appointed closets. Pepper, for all his genteel style, literally and figuratively lives downtown.

One day in the summer of 1981, a man named Paul Popham came up to Pepper. "My friends are dying of something," Popham said. "Would you help?" The disease was AIDS, and the organization created to combat it was Gay Men's Health Crisis. At a time when fear, ignorance, and anger threatened to thwart even the smallest effort, Pepper agreed to help promote GMHC's first big benefit—calling his friends to convince them to buy tickets, asking them to personally attend, and to spread the word about the event. That performance of the Ringling Brothers Barnum and Bailey Circus in a sold-out Madison Square Garden was the start of many successful GMHC fundraisers. Pepper remains active in the organization to this day as co-chair of the president's council.

Pepper and several other men of means have formed the Stonewall Foundation, which provides grassroots lesbian and gay organizations with the seed money and savvy they need to grow and become financially independent. Yet charity begins at home, and Pepper's philanthropy is catching: His mother has become the doyenne of efforts against AIDS in the Pepper hometown of Greensboro, North Carolina. Like her son, she offers not just cash, but time. "It's a reverse of *Driving Miss Daisy*," says Pepper. "There's my little seventy-five-year-old mother driving her car, and in the back seat is a Black lady with AIDS, on her way to a doctor's appointment."

Though he will always decline an ovation, Pepper and his ilk ensure that the gay show goes on. "It's been my privilege," he says, "to know so many amazing people who have done so much, so unconditionally—rich and poor, men and women, all colors." For gay men and lesbians, those doers include Jim Pepper—*and* his mother.

Jim Pepper is a total joy to work with. He is outspoken, unpredictable, and always very direct —generous and self-effacing: a very welcome and refreshing combination. I'm proud to call him a friend as well as a colleague.

—Jeff Soref

GMHC

16

Photographed by David Morgan

Jewelle Gomez

AUTHOR

It was standing room only the first night I heard it, Ntozake Shange's For Colored Girls Who Have Considered Suicide/When The Rainbow Is Enuf. And I decided to go back again. And again. But the first night I was just blown away by the performers, the ideas, the portraits of women as powerful, women taking care of each other. Women's stories were important. That was the turning point.

It wasn't until Jewelle Gomez saw *Colored Girls* that she realized she could write about what she knew. "All of a sudden I could write about lesbians," she says, "and the women that worked with my grandmother cleaning office buildings." Gomez had always thought of her life as rich and vital but had never seen it reflected before, not as it was in *Colored Girls,* and though she had been writing most of her life, it had just never occurred to her to write about her own life, or the world she knew. "I thought I should be constructing heterosexual romances!" she says, "None of them worked, of course. I had no idea of what would be a good plot, who would be a good character. I had *no idea.*"

There is no way to overstate the effect Shange had on Gomez and on her work. "There was a rawness about Ntozake's writing. A vitality," says Gomez. "She was a poet. Her stories were vibrant, rather than kitchen sink dramas. Women alone on a stage, no name, just the color of their dresses was enough. They blossomed with the essence of who they were." Gomez draws her creative impulses from a world centered around women—women whose stories she has seen, who are of interest, of importance. "I didn't have to write television dramas," she says. "I wanted to write what I know."

Gomez is busily adapting for the stage her critically well-received work about a lesbian vampire, *The Gilda Stories.* "I write with the audience in my head," she says, "That is, my friends and family. I want to create people that the women and men in my neighborhood would recognize." She is inventing characters who are very ordinary people that end up doing extraordinary things. She sees that as the definition of being heroic.

Living in San Francisco with her partner Dr. Diane Sabin, Gomez writes and teaches at New College and Menlo College, and her books include *The Lipstick Papers, Flamingoes and Bears,* and *Forty-three Septembers.* She has clear beliefs about where her work fits into the world. "Rather than getting my book on the women's studies syllabus," she says, "I enjoy thinking about seeing someone read my book on the subway. I want ordinary people to be reading me and finding out what I think lesbian feminism is and see it as some kind of alternative universe that they could safely go to."

Gomez is as Lorraine Hansberry. Young, gifted and Black; she is also a major literary and activist voice for our time.

—Victoria Brownworth
THE ADVOCATE

18

Photographed by Tee Corinne

Rob Sandoval and Bill Martin

PARENTS OF HARRISON MARTIN-SANDOVAL

We are raising our son to see that our life is exceptional rather than unusual. We think this is an exceptional way to raise a child in any type of community, whether gay or straight.

Bill Martin and Rob Sandoval were in the midst of reconfiguring their household in a small condominium, the bulk of their possessions having been removed to storage. Nearby, their spacious house in the Los Feliz district of Los Angeles was being reconstructed following the devastating 1994 Northridge earthquake. It would take a year or more to rebuild—but they took nature's unpredictability in stride. "It may not be the most original quote you've ever heard," says Martin, assessing the trauma, "but one thing my father taught me was that when life presents you with lemons, make lemonade. That's all we could do here."

Martin is founder and executive director of an adult daycare center and Sandoval is a municipal court commissioner, and together they have a natural instinct for weathering unpredictable jolts. Twelve years into their relationship, after five years of soul-searching discussions about raising a child, they braved their fears and the odds, and contacted an adoption attorney. They knew the adoption market was competitive and assumed it would be at least a year or two before a suitable match could be found, but within two weeks an expectant mother was located and negotiations began. Suddenly they were on the ride of their lives—the parenting track—which they recount with joy and not a trace of regret. Martin and Sandoval were chosen by the birth-mother over several straight couples due to the emotional stability of their relationship and their resolve to raise a child in a wholesome, spiritual environment. The ensuing months were often stress-filled and uncertain, but the couple's commitment never wavered. "The turning point for us," they concur, "was the delight in hearing the words, 'You are now the parents.'" On September 18, 1992, Harrison Martin-Sandoval was delivered into his parents' waiting arms, and they cut the umbilical cord themselves. "Harrison's birth was the most spiritual and euphoric event in our lives," says Sandoval.

These gay parents are heroes of the twenty-first century, pioneers redefining the parameters of the American family. After having anticipated and analyzed every aspect of how this experience would impact their lives, Martin and Sandoval keep a refreshingly clear-sighted, simple outlook. "'Where is Poppa? Where is Daddy?' That's all Harrison cares about. And as long as he knows we're here, he's happy," they say. "But it's important to us that Harrison knows we feel fortunate to be his parents. We feel like we're the lucky ones."

Bill and Rob earn our respect, not only because of their special status as parents, but because of their exceptional ability to consider how their decisions will impact both their lives and the lives of others. It is a love that extends far beyond whatever challenges they may encounter.

—Tony Alfano
CLINICAL PSYCHOLOGIST

Photographed by Honowitz
Courtesy Martin/Sandoval

Bruce Hayes

OLYMPIC GOLD MEDAL SWIMMER
Being a swimmer who's an out gay man means that I have more than water to buoy me up.

By the time he was twenty, Bruce Hayes had already appeared on the cover of *Swimming World;* at twenty-one he had been featured with the rest of his U.S. Olympic swimming relay team on the cover of *Vanity Fair,* surrounding Raquel Welch. "But the more public I became, the more frightened I was that my secret—being gay—would be revealed," he says. "It got to the point where the most comfortable place for me was in the pool." Hayes anchored the American team, beating out his West German competitor by four-hundredths of a second to take the gold in the 1984 Olympics in Los Angeles. The UCLA junior had become a world champion—but he had yet to accept himself as a man.

That process began after the Olympics when Hayes started fashioning a life for himself to go along with his gold medal—when he finally tasted the freedom he had denied himself during his years of disciplined swimming. "Because I was closeted and single-minded about my swimming," he says, "I thought coming out, even if it were only a few tentative steps, would interfere with my training and competition." In his remaining years at UCLA, he began to slowly explore what it means to be a gay man. On the night before a family wedding, his father accidentally came upon some letters that revealed the fact that Hayes is gay. The discovery provoked a crisis greater than any Hayes had ever faced. "I felt like I had lost my family," he says. "Like I was totally alone. And I still had no gay community to connect to." But after the shock wore off, his parents came to terms with it, and supported his choice to come out as a gay Olympian. He also kept swimming, but on his own terms: winning seven gold medals in Vancouver in 1990 at Gay Games III.

Hayes now lives in New York, where he is a public relations executive actively involved in the production and promotion of Gay Games IV. Ten years after his breathtaking Olympic win in Los Angeles, Hayes is anchoring Team New York Aquatics and helping to anchor the Games themselves—performing with his whole heart, the way real champions do.

Bruce Hayes is an excellent example of what the Gay Games are showing the world: gays and lesbians are out there in the sports world, just like we are out there in the rest of society. His visibility and commitment have been an inspiration to thousands of Gay Games participants around the world.

—Jay Hill
GAY GAMES

23

Karen Clark

STATE LEGISLATOR

I got elected in 1980 on the same day as Ronald Reagan. That's where our similarities begin and end.

In 1993 grassroots momentum propelled Karen Clark to the sweetest victory of her fourteen-year career as a Minnesota Representative, when protection for gay men and lesbians was added to the state civil rights statute. Clark had organized for an entire year before the introduction of the bill into the legislature. By the time it came up for a vote, almost all of Minnesota's major churches, labor organizations, the League of Women Voters, and ethnic minority organizations were in support. She even succeeded in getting the approval of Lutheran and Roman Catholic bishops.

"Many of the legislators were so disgusted by the hatred, bigotry, and misinformation put out by the right-wing fundamentalists," says Clark. "They would say to me, 'Politically, I probably shouldn't vote for this bill. But, if I didn't know there was a need for it before, the incredible level of hatred and bigotry I've heard over the phone from people calling me in opposition has convinced me that I have to support it.'" In a bipartisan effort, the bill received eleven more votes than required, a margin Clark considers a major victory. No one had more reason to be pleased than Clark when Republican Governor Arne Carlson signed it into law.

But Clark didn't become the longest-serving openly lesbian or gay elected public official in America by concerning herself only with lesbian and gay issues. She serves an inner city district on the south side of Minneapolis of primarily lower-income people, with many elderly, disabled, struggling young families, African-Americans, and southeast Asian immigrants, along with one of the highest concentrations of Native Americans of any urban area in the United States. "It's a wonderful district to represent," says Clark. "I'm able to do exactly what I believe in. I get to work on real survival issues: jobs, housing, affordable health care, and civil rights issues of every kind."

When Karen Clark first ran for public office in 1980, she encountered homophobia and sexism at every turn. Karen never reacted with bitterness; instead, she invited her detractors to lunch and won them over one by one. She is one of the most caring and compassionate people I know. The homeless, the disenfranchised, people of color, and people with disabilities all have a wonderful friend in Karen. I am proud to serve in the Minnesota legislature with her. I am also proud to be her friend.

—Senator Allan Spear

PRESIDENT OF THE MINNESOTA STATE SENATE

David Hockney

ARTIST

The moment you can learn to deal with homosexuality in art, it's quite an exciting moment, just as in a sense when people 'come out' it's quite an exciting moment. It means they become aware of their desires and deal with them in a remarkably honest way.

David Hockney has been dealing honestly with his desires from the beginning of his career, for his discovery of his sexuality was virtually simultaneous with his coming out. While a student at London's Royal Academy of Art from 1959 to 1962, he produced such paintings as *Queer, Bertha Alias Bernie, Doll Boy* and *We Two Boys Together Clinging* (one of several debts to poet Walt Whitman). Speaking of his early work, Hockney says, "What one must remember about some of these pictures is that they were partly propaganda of something I felt hadn't been propagandized, especially among students, as a subject: homosexuality. I felt it should be done. Nobody else would use it as a subject." Hockney used it, but even in his student days he was much less a maker of gay art than an openly gay artist mining autobiographical material to explore stylistic possibilities.

Already a celebrated painter in England, he moved to California in 1964 and quickly established an American reputation in work that has given us some of the most vivid images of our culture: the flat, unpeopled houses of Los Angeles, the young men showering and sleeping together, the Beverly Hills housewives and art collectors, the portraits of domestic couples, and, of course, the famous swimming pools. At age fifty-seven, Hockney has long been an internationally celebrated artist whose work is sought by collectors and museums the world over. He is also a man of strong social conscience who donates work to AIDS benefits and speaks out against censorship and sexual discrimination.

An ardent individualist who once remarked that his father "taught me not to care what the neighbors think," Hockney has never followed artistic fashions; going his own eccentric way, he has instead created them. In barely three decades he has produced groundbreaking work in painting, graphics, stage design, photography, and most recently, computer art. Hockney has turned Los Angeles into a subject for painting, stretched the boundaries of photocollage, shown us the miracles of Chinese scroll painting, inspired a reevaluation of Picasso's final decade, and got us thinking about Cubism again. He has increased our joy, and his career continues to be one of the great aesthetic and intellectual adventures of our time. Hooray for David Hockney!

This is a terrible show. People stand around looking at these paintings for hours.

—Museum Guard
AT THE METROPOLITAN
MUSEUM OF ART'S
HOCKNEY
RETROSPECTIVE

Margarethe Cammermeyer

FORMER U.S. ARMY COLONEL

It's my most fervent hope that nobody has to go through a witch-hunt or this sort of ordeal and exposure ever again. If we're the last ones, then it will have been worth going through it.

She was the head nurse of a medical intensive care unit, then of a neurological intensive care unit during her fourteen month tour of duty in Vietnam. At the age of forty-two she was the highest ranked woman in the Army National Guard. In 1985 she was named the Veteran Administration Nurse of the Year. Yet on July 14, 1991, Colonel Margarethe Cammermeyer, a woman who had won both a bronze and a silver star, faced the four members of the Army and National Guard Officers Board as Colonel Patsy Thompson told her, "I totally believe you are one of the great Americans, Margarethe, and I've admired you for a long time and all that you've done for the Army National Guard." Then Thompson formally discharged the decorated twenty-seven-year veteran from the military.

One thing is perfectly clear: Cammermeyer was not just any soldier, nor did she leave the army she loved because she wanted to. During a routine investigation for a security clearance, she had admitted that she was a lesbian, feeling it was time to simply tell the truth. Cammermeyer then became the highest ranking officer in the military to fight the ban on lesbians and gay men serving in the armed forces.

Born in Norway to a family involved with the resistance movement that had fought the Nazis during World War II, nine-year-old Cammermeyer and her family came to the United States in 1952. In college, she signed up for the Army Student Nurse Program exactly thirty years to the day before she would be booted out. The mother of four children, Cammermeyer divorced her husband of sixteen years in 1981 and began to come to terms with her sexuality. "In some ways, because of my upbringing, I was probably as homophobic as everyone else," she says. "We give lip service to the concept that just because one is homosexual, it has nothing to do with being different from everyone else. Yet I perceived that other people were going to look at me differently, so I acted differently."

We are senselessly losing an outstanding individual.

—William Booth Gardner
WASHINGTON GOVERNOR

Though the governor of Washington personally lobbied Defense Secretary Richard Cheney on Cammermeyer's behalf, the military did not care. The expulsion of homosexuals would not abate—even for an officer of such rare ability and accomplishment. Cammermeyer has vowed to fight back though, and is suing in federal court with the help of Lambda Legal and Educational Defense Fund, with her children behind her one hundred percent. "I'm not a young private," she says, "and the Army can't beat up on me." More power to her.

29

Phill Wilson

ACTIVIST

For African Americans, 'home' means a sanctuary from a world that, on racism alone, can destroy us. You go downtown and they call you a nigger. When you go back home, your mother, your sister, and your brother, they know how it feels. But when I go downtown and get called a faggot, even if my family is supportive, I still have to spend time teaching them how it feels.

As an African-American gay man Phill Wilson embodies American culture clash—part of that so-called "intersection" adjoining race and sexuality. When he speaks of the need for African-American lesbians and gay men to "go home," the meaning seems clear, but for a white-collar, middle-class, African-American gay man with AIDS, "home" isn't always easy to find.

Wilson is the high-profile director of public policy for AIDS Project Los Angeles, the country's second largest AIDS service organization. Some may feel he is susceptible to being discounted as merely a "suit," but Wilson's suit, while derided by some, is his Trojan horse. His disarming handsomeness and poise are quite capable of concealing an unreckoned bone of contention, such as when he asserts to majority white lesbian and gay gatherings that "the gay rights movement cannot mean the rights of white gay men to oppress us in the way their straight counterparts do."

His lack of cynicism at such times is most affecting, and many feel it epitomizes Wilson's leadership; a fearlessness to call the white gay community on its racism and the Black community on its homophobia. His dogged insistence on reaching out to bridge the divides of race, gender, and sexuality—not merely as a reflex, but because of conscience–is the truly radical impulse toward synthesis and community.

In ten years of activism Wilson has either founded, co-founded, or served as the principal emissary of one grass-roots group after another, most based in Los Angeles, where he lives. It went without saying, that when President Clinton invited gay and lesbian leaders for a White House tête-à-tête in 1993, the contingent designated Wilson as one of its spokespeople. "I worry about being honest, consistent, fair, and open," he says. "But I don't worry about being right."

Phill Wilson has proven over the past decade that he represents, and has the ability to translate, the frustrations of several different communities into a coherent and influential message, which is why people respond to him.

—Mario Cooper
AIDS ACTION COUNCIL

Pat Norman

STONEWALL 25 CO-CHAIR

Back when I was a Navy wife with four children and still wanted to be a heterosexual, a Navy psychiatrist unintentionally convinced me to come out of the closet. He offered to 'cure' me and told me that I could go into the hospital and have electric shock therapy—that after sixty days I would be heterosexual. He must have been crazier than I was to even suggest such a thing. I realized that I wasn't the person with problems, and that's when I turned my life around.

I've known and admired Pat Norman for a long time. She is an effective and accomplished advocate for her constituencies. I chose Pat to be the '1992 Woman of the Year' for my legislative district and she graciously accepted. A woman of immense integrity, Pat is a valued friend.

—Willie Brown, Jr.
CALIFORNIA SPEAKER OF
THE ASSEMBLY

Being homosexual was still seen as a pathology when Pat Norman decided to come out of the closet in the late 1960s. After their divorce, her husband won custody of their four young children because the court believed that Norman could not possibly be a fit parent. But she knew that there was no way she could deny her lesbian identity, and she became involved in lesbian issues—first in Philadelphia, and then in San Francisco—and she regained custody of her children by default when her ex-husband abandoned them.

Lesbian mothers weren't exactly commonplace in those days (never mind "chic"), so Norman helped organize the Lesbian Mothers Union at the 1971 Daughters of Bilitis (DOB) conference in Los Angeles in order to better the lives of lesbian mothers and their children. "We met with a lot of resistance," says Norman, "not only from the DOB, but when we marched in the L. A. gay pride parade, some people thought we were a joke–they just couldn't 'conceive' of lesbians being mothers."

But social activism comes naturally to Norman. "I just have this passion for equality and justice," she says. "I can remember walking picket lines with my parents when I was four years old. I was much older before I discovered that everyone didn't do that. My mother, Maude B. Richardson, even seconded the nomination of Dwight D. Eisenhower for president at the Republican National Convention in 1956." During her almost two decades at the San Francisco Department of Health, Norman trained health care professionals to deal competently and sensitively with gay, lesbian, and bisexual health issues, and worked to create a gay clients' bill of rights. Once the AIDS epidemic hit, she was instrumental in creating a system of AIDS related services that became a national model.

In the many images of Norman that define her activism, there is perhaps one that is forever etched in the minds of Californians: She and her partner of eleven years, attorney and activist Karen Norman, appeared in a billboard that was placed throughout the state which featured Pat with her hand on Karen's stomach five days before Karen gave birth to their son Zach. The headline read simply, "Another Traditional Family."

Photograph Courtesy Norman

33

Written by Michael Van Duzer

Virginia Apuzzo

POLITICAL LEADER AND ACTIVIST

One of the most profoundly painful aspects of life for hundreds and thousands of gays and lesbians has been the forced exile brought on by being rejected from our families, and those institutions and supports that are our birthrights as members of our respective communities.

At two in the morning, only hours before the twentieth anniversary of Martin Luther King Jr.'s March on Washington, Virginia Apuzzo was fighting hard to prove that gay and lesbian rights are civil rights. For nearly two hours she had been on a conference call with Coretta Scott King and other organizers of a commemorative march called the Coalition of Conscience. Exhaustion had taken its toll on everyone's already overtaxed nerves, but the organizers remained adamantly opposed to including a lesbian or gay speaker. "The excuses they were giving sounded just like those that were leveled against Black Americans that provoked Dr. King to write his *Letter From a Birmingham Jail*," says Apuzzo. "They were going on about how 'the coalition is fragile' and 'The church groups won't understand.' I felt such a sense of irony repeating the words of Martin Luther King back to his wife."

Late nights and hard fights are nothing new to Virginia Apuzzo, a longtime activist and currently the Executive Deputy Commissioner of the New York State Division of Housing and Community Renewal. At the 1980 Democratic National Convention she co-authored the first lesbian and gay civil rights platform adopted by a major political party in America. As vice-chair of the New York State AIDS Advisory Council she fought for PWA rights and negotiated with the Social Security Administration to insure benefits. And as executive director of the National Gay and Lesbian Task Force from 1982 through 1985 she was instrumental in getting the movement better organized and more visible, and pushing forward the cause.

The morning after that difficult phone call with the Coalition of Conscience, Apuzzo made no mention of the heated, behind-the-scenes struggle where she had finally prevailed. She proudly took her place at a Washington D.C. press conference saying, "We come home this day renewed in our determination to confront racism and sexism in our own community, revitalized in our determination to forge coalitions, and recommitted to building a movement that will strengthen that network of mutuality being commemorated this week-end." As she stood before the assembled crowd, it all looked so easy—Apuzzo was poised, strong and articulate. But don't let that fool you. Virginia Apuzzo knows what it takes to fight the good fight and how much it costs to tell the truth. She just keeps doing it anyway.

Twenty years ago we had a March on Washington and one year later we saw the passage of the Civil Rights Act of 1964. It's time to amend the law and include the rights of lesbians and gay men.

—Coretta Scott King

Photographed by Rick Gerharter

Richard Rouilard

JOURNALIST

There is a national distaste for gay and lesbian rights. In newsrooms around the country most editors will not equate the gay and lesbian struggle with that of Blacks, Hispanics, or other minorities. And the way gay journalism has been, gay and lesbian issues were incidental to mainstream America. But my position is that good journalism is good journalism.

When Los Angeles journalist Richard Rouilard took the helm of *The Advocate* in 1990, his mission was nothing short of putting gay and lesbian issues on the national radar screen. His very first cover featured a lipstick-enhanced photograph of Senator Jessie Helms as "Sissy of the Year," and the mainstream news media couldn't help but take notice. "My task at *The Advocate* was to bring a new standard of reporting, because I had a sense that the community was not being covered," says Rouilard, who quickly transformed the twenty-five-year-old publication from a "gay *Town & Country*" to, as the publication's masthead promised, "The National Gay and Lesbian Newsmagazine."

Under Rouilard's direction, *The Advocate* aggressively tackled such subjects as gay and lesbian teen suicide, homophobia in Hollywood, and the ongoing AIDS crisis. It acquired a politically charged edge, providing a forum for controversial columnists like queer-activist Michelangelo Signorile, and branching beyond its traditional gay-White-male audience to cover lesbians and people of color. And *The Advocate* got the beat on a number of juicy stories that left the mainstream media playing catch-up: k.d. lang's revelation that she is a lesbian; the controversial outing of former Assistant Secretary of Defense Pete Williams; and a *particularly* racy interview with Madonna.

Rouilard, a one-time gay rights attorney who co-founded National Gay Rights Advocates, broke into journalism in 1980 with a weekly gossip column for a department store "advertorial" under the nom de plume *Bunny Mars* (ever-flamboyant, Rouilard had wanted to call the column *The Ears of Bunny Mars* after the campy Faye Dunaway thriller). He went on to become an editor at *L.A. Style Magazine,* then a society columnist and senior editor at the *Los Angeles Herald Examiner,* before being recruited for the top job at *The Advocate.*

After leaving the magazine in 1992, Rouilard is now a senior editorial consultant at the *Los Angeles Times,* where he says, "I've been able to take my experience in gay journalism and translate it to a different venue." As a member of the National Lesbian and Gay Journalists Association, which honored him in October 1993 for his career achievements, Rouilard continues to play an active role in making fair coverage of gay and lesbian issues a priority in newsrooms across the nation.

Since Richard Rouilard became editor in June 1990, The Advocate has been anything but boring. Rouilard injected an aggressive, news-oriented flavor. He is 'The Voice of Gay Rights.'

—TIME MAGAZINE

The Reverend Troy Perry

SPIRITUAL LEADER AND AUTHOR

We don't want to destroy the National Council of Churches. We just want the fellowship of other Christians. Sometimes it's harder to come out as a Christian in the gay community than to come out as a gay or lesbian in the straight world.

The Reverend Troy Perry's evangelistic commitment to proclaiming God's inclusive love has transformed many lives. When there was mostly silence within religious circles, his was one of the first voices to arise, denouncing oppression, standing for justice, building communities of faith.

—The Reverend Bill Johnson
UNITED CHURCH
OF CHRIST

The National Council of Churches just can't stop debating. In November 1993 they deferred until 1995 making a decision about the application of the Universal Fellowship of Metropolitan Community Churches, a Protestant denomination founded by the Reverend Troy Perry. MCC does not diverge from other Christian bodies in its theology and would easily blend with the Council's other members save for one thing: MCC contends that homosexual love is neither immoral nor prohibited by the Bible when scriptures are authentically interpreted. The fact that the National Council of Churches hasn't yet said no is probably a miracle in and of itself.

That MCC exists at all is the result of years of dedication, demonstration, patience, and love by the Reverend Perry, who began his vocation at age thirteen and was a licensed Baptist minister at age fifteen. He married and had two sons, but his idyllic life began to unravel when he moved to Southern California and experienced an "uneasy" coming out as a gay man. He divorced and joined the Army, where he had what he declares a divine revelation "that you could be a Christian and a gay person, too!" He returned to Los Angeles and, with a small band of twelve, founded the original Metropolitan Community Church.

It was tough going at first for Perry. He endured frequent public fastings and often chained himself to telephone poles—all to call attention to the plight of gay persons attempting to have a place of Christian worship. His first church was torched, its leaders were frequently harassed, and members often attended services fearing reprisals from Fundamentalist groups. But the MCC concept grew stronger in the face of adversity and new churches sprouted all over America.

Perry lives in Los Angeles, preaches all over the world, and continues to guide the church he loves. He has written a highly praised autobiography, *The Lord is My Shepherd and He Knows I'm Gay,* and a sequel, *Don't be Afraid Anymore,* and has also produced the acclaimed video *God, Gays & The Gospel: This is Our Story.* Today there are over two hundred fifty odd churches worldwide and UFMCC membership is at about thirty thousand. Yet it has been a difficult and challenging decade. MCC has been dramatically affected by AIDS—close to five thousand members have died from the disease. Still, this crisis has brought many new worshippers who seek the spiritual comfort that Perry and the church he founded hope to provide.

Ayofemi Folayan

WORDSMITH AND ACTORVIST

Growing up a lesbian in a family full of Pentecostal ministers was like being an Eskimo who landed in the middle of the Sahara Desert.

Coming out in pre-Stonewall Boston wasn't simply a choice for Ayofemi Folayan—like deciding whether or not she preferred a different flavor of ice cream. As a teenager, she was caught *en flagrante delicto* with another girl and was quickly taken to the church she had grown up in, where the family and community she trusted as a child laid on hands to remove the demons that possessed her. When she "persisted" in claiming her sexual identity, she was thrown out of the church and into a psychiatric hospital. This was a time when lesbianism was still listed in the psychiatric canon as a mental illness.

Standing up for her love of women in the face of such tremendous opposition and rejection was a brave and irrevocable act. It was the beginning of a life-long struggle that honed her will, not only to survive but to thrive. This turning point engendered her lasting commitment to the basic human rights of dignity and inclusivity for all people.

Leaping into a gay and lesbian community that wasn't ready for an African-American lesbian with disabilities, Folayan felt caught between two worlds—a woman truly on the edge of her time. She discovered that the battle for recognition and inclusion was far from over, and began to find her deeply imbedded activist spirit—raising her voice through writing and performance work. She used her life story to approach issues of sexism, racism, and ableism, writing of the strength everyone has inside to fight and unlearn oppression in all its guises.

In performance work such as *Tri-Sections,* a nationally touring piece, Folayan eloquently confronts what it means to be an African- American, a lesbian, and a woman with lupus and cancer. Her commitment to own all of her self, and to create places that are safe for her to be all of who she is, has enabled her to build bridges of understanding within the African-American political community, the disability rights movement, and among gay men and lesbians. Today, in writing classes at several gay and lesbian centers, she continues to empower others by teaching the healing power of the word to reclaim and uphold all of one's identity.

Ayofemi creates a community full of possibilities. She explores and shares her complex identity while inspiring and entertaining us. Hers is a powerful and articulate voice.

—Tim Miller
PERFORMANCE ARTIST

Written by Elizabeth Randolph

Katherine Acey

ACTIVIST

Activism requires a constant leap of faith in myself and others, and the openness to change and be changed. Personal and political transformation is about reflection and action—about keeping my heart and mind on what I believe and on whom I love.

In the fall of 1991, Katherine Acey presented her executive director's report at the monthly meeting of the Astraea Foundation's board of directors, answered questions, then politely excused herself. She was off to sit on a panel with women of Jewish and Arab descent who had visited the West Bank and Gaza Strip to witness for themselves the treatment of Palestinians in the occupied territories, and to dialogue with other feminists in the area. Just a typical hectic schedule for this "activist's activist," a woman of tenacity with a keen ability to bridge people and issues. "As a feminist," she says, "my politics are very much defined by looking at the big picture, seeing how our lives intersect, and working for change in that context, no matter where I choose to focus my attention at any given moment."

Acey's work is often focused on affirming and acknowledging the existence and experience of lesbians, not only in the country at large, but also within the lesbian community. In fact, it wasn't until 1990, when the Astraea Foundation, founded thirteen years earlier to empower women and girls, "came out" as the National Lesbian Action Foundation. It was a step that reflected the contributions and needs of the lesbian community, which received only a fraction of the meager foundation monies awarded to women's and girls' projects each year. "It was a way of saying we are committed to taking the leadership in articulating the needs of lesbians," says Acey, "that we are ready to act on a vision and take matters into our own hands."

The Astraea Foundation is now busy strengthening the infrastructure that will support that vision. Under Acey's leadership, Astraea recently received one of the largest grants ever awarded to a lesbian organization by a private foundation—a capacity-building grant for $400,000 from the Joyce Mertz-Gilmore Foundation. Acey knows that the money is important, not only for its practical benefits—such as helping to create a national advisory board, hire the appropriate staff, build an endowment, and create a strategic plan that will take Astraea into the next century—but for more symbolic reasons, too. It is an affirmation of the organization, and of what the organization is about: lesbians working autonomously and in coalition with allies for the purpose of social justice.

Kathy Acey is a tireless organizer, ally, and kindred spirit—a true visionary who has inspired, challenged, and brought hope to countless numbers of women throughout our nation.

—Marjorie J. Hill, Ph.D
PUBLIC HEALTH OFFICIAL

Robert LaFosse

DANCER AND CHOREOGRAPHER

Don't do anything you don't want to do. Don't be a bank clerk, if that isn't what you want. Don't set-tle. Don't give yourself a time limit either. If you really want something, pure determination is more important than sheer talent.

When acclaimed dancer and choreographer Robert LaFosse published his autobiography, *Nothing to Hide,* in 1987, it was a frank account of his struggle to become a dancer while trying to define his mascu-linity as a gay man, despite the social pressures that say dancing is for "sissies." He received a letter from a counselor working with teenage runaways, who wrote that LaFosse's book had inspired some of them and given them courage. "I wish I'd had a book like that," says LaFosse. "I didn't have any gay role models except for my brother Edmund."

LaFosse was lucky, though, in that he had supportive parents and a strong teacher in Beaumont, Texas—learning not only ballet, but tap, jazz and acrobatics. Going to New York at age eighteen was a big risk, but his talent got him into the American Ballet Theatre on his first audition. After three years in the corps de ballet, he made a breakthrough as a principal dancer in *The Prodigal Son* on ABT's 1980 opening night at Washington's Kennedy Center. He describes it as a highlight of his life, and he danced many major roles with this great company in the following years.

In 1985 the first ballet he choreographed was performed at the Metropolitan Opera House for an AIDS gala featuring Baryshnikov, Chita Rivera, the New York City Gay Men's Chorus, and Bette Midler. He went on to premiere his highly acclaimed *I Have My Own Room* at New York City Ballet in 1992. It was a deeply personal work in which he danced the role of a young man coming to terms with himself and the world around him. Between ballet seasons, LaFosse has also starred on Broadway, replacing an injured dancer in Bob Fosse's *Dancin',* and later using everything he learned back in Beaumont to win a Tony Award nomination as a featured performer in *Jerome Robbins' Broadway.*

Now in his mid-thirties, and a star with the New York City Ballet, LaFosse is choreographing more ballets. After losing many friends and colleagues to AIDS, he is working to fight the disease by raising money at benefits like the one he recently organized, *A Demand Performance.* He still keeps the discipline of the ballet dancer, often starting his day with a 10:00 a.m. class and finishing it at 11:00 p.m. following a performance—imbuing his life and his work with a sense of freedom and truth.

Robert LaFosse's dancing unites athletic vigor with a sense of style and characterization. He makes every role look different—and convincing. Now, as a developing choreographer, he brings to his ballets the same flair and theatrical intelligence that have distinguished his performances.

—Jack Anderson
NEW YORK TIMES

Frank Andrade

BULLRIDER

I'm going to learn to ride bulls, I'm going to compete in the rodeo, and I'm going to win!

It took him three years of hard work, but he did it. Frank Andrade, a gymnast and swimmer, was accustomed to physical challenges. But when he came home from seeing his first gay rodeo in Phoenix, Arizona in 1987, he knew this was another challenge he would have to conquer. He went to a ranch in Narco, California to get some experience. Determination and discipline would take him just where he wanted to go, he believed, and he didn't let anything get in his way—even when he tested HIV-positive. In 1990, Andrade won his bull riding buckle in San Diego. It wasn't much of a surprise to anyone who knew him.

Yet Andrade wasn't only a bullrider. He went on to Pomona College, hoping to become a writer. "I want to write cogently about subjects that need to be addressed," he wrote in his application. "Health care for everyone; instilling young children with a sense of fiscal, environmental, and ethical responsibility; affordable housing; and most importantly, teaching ourselves, and our young citizens to see people as individuals regardless of ethnicity, religion, preference of mate, physical challenge, or any other trait that doesn't hurt others, and adds to the variety of our species."

Less than a year before his death in 1992, and while still a college student, Andrade joined the Being Alive speakers bureau in Los Angeles, and was soon a leader of the group. He talked to any organization or group of people who would listen, telling of his experiences as an HIV-positive person—abandonment by family and friends, social stigmatization, and health care difficulties. At one point, Michael Dwiggins, director of Being Alive, asked Andrade if he would speak to a group that had specifically asked for someone visibly ill, so that people would learn not to fear the physical signs of the disease. At that time, Andrade had Kaposi's Sarcoma lesions on his face. He put aside his personal reservations and agreed to do it. It was typical of his bravery. He evoked a tremendously supportive response from the group that day—no one thought he was a victim. And no matter how much life bucked beneath him, Andrade hung on until the last bell rang.

Who was Frank Andrade? He was a man who decided to accept consciously, and with dignity, that the end of his life was at hand. No struggle. No complaint. Just acceptance. I stand in awe of his courage and truth. Who was Frank Andrade? In case you have forgotten, he was your brother.

—Michael Lawrence
Dwiggins
BEING ALIVE

Howard J. Brown, M.D.

GAY RIGHTS ACTIVIST

Acknowledging that I am a gay man in an address to some six hundred physicians at a symposium on human sexuality in 1973 ended my life of fear. But more importantly, it helped to open up a public dialogue on homosexuality, focusing on the problems and rights of homosexuals.

Howard Brown cared deeply for people and was remarkably sensitive to their individual qualities. That sensitivity suffuses his book, making it all at once a poignant memoir of the man himself and a powerful contribution to the more humane society he worked so hard to bring into being.

—Martin Duberman

AUTHOR AND SCHOLAR

At 3:00 a.m. on June 28, 1969, the police raided the Stonewall Inn at 53 Christopher Street, only a four minute walk from Dr. Howard Brown's Greenwich Village apartment in New York. Like many other gay men and lesbians, Brown began to draw an important comparison in his mind. "My front windows were open," he said, "and I could hear the shouting. It brought to mind every civil rights struggle I had ever witnessed." Brown had been quite active in the early civil rights movement, but had never thought to relate his own struggle as a gay man to that of those in the Black community. He had accepted the common notion in society at the time that to be homosexual was to be consigned to a life of hiding and of fear.

In 1968 Brown had been Mayor John V. Lindsay's Health Services Administrator for two years when a rumor began to circulate that he was gay. Most people found it difficult to believe that a man as successful as Brown could possibly be homosexual. In fact, in assuring another city official not to pay attention to gossip, Mayor Lindsay was heard to say, "Don't worry, some people will say anything. A few weeks ago they were saying that Howard Brown was a homosexual!"—as if that were the most impossible thing imaginable. But Brown was terrified by his brush with being exposed. "I saw myself accused of being myself, and I felt utterly defenseless," he said, and could not bring himself to be open about his sexual orientation.

But five years later when he publicly came out, he had recently had a heart attack. "Since my life seemed possibly finite, I thought I had better act soon," he said. "I knew there was one legacy I wanted to leave, to help in some way to free future generations of homosexuals from the agony of secrecy." His 1973 announcement made the front page of the *New York Times* because as a former city official, a respected professor at New York University's School of Public Administration and its School of Medicine, Brown confounded stereotypes of gay men. He went on to become one of the most respected homosexual spokespersons of the 1970s; his groundbreaking book, *Familiar Faces, Hidden Lives,* was one of the first chronicles of what it was like to be a gay man in America. In tribute to the remarkable effect he had on the gay community, a Chicago health clinic for homosexual research and casework was renamed the Howard Brown Clinic after his death in 1975.

Tim Taylor

VIBRATIONAL ARTIST

I find color to be very joyful; happy. Vibrational Art has within it a consciousness of joy because those are the things which help us not only to survive, but to be happy. If we're constantly worrying and considering dreadful thoughts, that's what we'll attract. I had always felt confined and restricted because of physical limitations and had to learn to be discriminating with my thoughts.

What a source of inspiration. Sometimes I can barely fathom the source of Tim Taylor's determination and consistent good cheer. And nothing—no bureaucrat, no system, no physical disability—is going to stand in his way.

—Jim Petzke

CALIFORNIA DEPUTY
ATTORNEY GENERAL

Life has a way of delivering gifts as well as challenges. When Tim Taylor was six years old, he contracted polio and was placed in an iron lung only a few months before the Sabin polio vaccine was introduced to the world. The polio left him unable to use his arms, but this talented visual artist was raised by parents who insisted he test himself in the world in spite of his physical handicaps. Taylor learned to paint with his feet—in an abstract, expressionistic style which he calls Vibrational Art; multiple-layered textures and vivid colors in a broad splatter/stroke style expressing "frozen energy."

Taylor's painting (the Vibrational Art and his more traditional landscapes) came to the attention of the prestigious Associations of Mouth and Foot Painters, World-Wide, which is based in Switzerland, and they awarded him a monthly stipend in order that he might continue his work. In addition, he has been exhibited in sites as varied as the West Hollywood City Hall, the Arts Center/Pasadena, and galleries in Los Angeles and Cleveland. He's a member of the Los Angeles County Museum of Art's Emerging Artists Program.

Before blossoming as a painter, Taylor developed a variety of interests, including studying acting at the famous Lee Strasberg Studio in Hollywood, attending the Self-Realization Fellowship Church, and becoming a member of the disability taskforce of the Alliance for Gay and Lesbian Artists in the Entertainment Industry (AGLA). "I afford myself visibility by participating in social activities within the gay community," he says. "I feel I have just as much right as any other gay person to have the opportunity to date, and be considered as a potential partner." Taylor is also a well-known advocate for disabled rights issues, co-founding the Performing Arts Theatre of the Handicapped (PATH) and helping to develop and create the media office for the California Governor's Committee for Employment of the Handicapped in 1979. Both organizations significantly encourage positive public attitudes toward persons with disabilities. He has taught Theatre Arts in college, and with his family is co-owner of Taylor Brothers Landscaping Company in Cleveland.

Photographed by Becky Villasenor

Luis Alfaro

WRITER AND PERFORMANCE ARTIST

My desire is memory, and yet I know it is not enough to just remember. I feel that my job as a writer is to be a documentarian. Record the losses. In a poem, maybe, but also in a rant.

Luis Alfaro stands at the front of a classroom, before thirty graduate playwriting students, and assigns the first exercise: they must criticize their parents. A hush descends over the room as bowed heads scribble furiously in the brief time allotted. All goes well, until Alfaro asks for people to share what they have written with the class. A student suddenly explodes out of his seat and heads for the door, screaming an irate, garbled protest. But Alfaro stops him, and calmly says, "You're free to go, but first articulate to the class why you're upset."

No stranger to people walking out in anger or disgust, Alfaro sees it happen sometimes with students in one of the many writing classes he teaches, or an uncomfortable audience member witnessing one of Alfaro's openly gay, openly Latino performance pieces. His response is always the same: "Tell me why." A native downtown Los Angeleno, a former heroin addict, and a union organizer who has been out since age sixteen, Alfaro understands that the ability to communicate your perspective, in your own voice, is the most valuable asset you have. It is also an opportunity rarely granted by society. He knows that, despite garnering critical acclaim and national recognition, his work is disturbing for some people simply because it addresses both his cultural and sexual identities. This soft-spoken man is adamant about not censoring or soft-pedaling his identity. And always, he returns to the question, "Why?"

Alfaro is uncomfortable with labeling his work as specifically Latino, or specifically queer. And the final form of what he calls his "memory plays"—the autobiographical works that he has written "in order to stay sane"—may be poetry, theatre, or performance art. As a writer, performer, director, producer, and teacher, he hungers for expression, and for finding the best means of channeling that expression. Whether in the role of collaborator, organizer, or mentor, he counsels others to stay with the hard questions: Who are you? What is your need? What is your desire? What do you have to say? What is your language? How do you speak? Because above all else, Alfaro knows, you must tell your story.

The more Luis deals with his Latino issues, his gay issues, the more universal his work is. I would not identify it as either gay or Latino. I would identify it as human.

—Michael Kearns
ACTOR AND ACTIVIST

Melissa Etheridge

SINGER

I understand that for celebrities and famous people, you're in the closet if you don't say who you are. It's different—you have to say it out loud. But every person I've worked with, every single person that is a friend, everybody who knows me in any way, knows that I am a lesbian, and has always known. My record company—everyone. I've never hidden that. It's just that when it came to the press, I didn't put it in my bio.

The weekend of President Clinton's Inauguration, Grammy Award-winning singer Melissa Etheridge was very popular. She sang for the Clintons and the Gores with Aretha Franklin, and again with the Rock the Vote crowd. But she made a bigger splash at the gay and lesbian Triangle Ball. Not only did Etheridge publicly acknowledge that she is a lesbian, she thrilled lesbians and gay men by joking around with k.d. lang as both kissed the heterosexual television star, Elvira, Mistress of the Dark, on the lips.

Etheridge discovered what being a lesbian was when she had a secret, intimate, but "natural" relationship with her best friend at age seventeen in Leavenworth, Kansas. She thought the two of them were the only ones until she went to college in Boston and met "a whole bunch of people who were just like me."

The most important coming out, though, was to her adored father, three years later. "I just wanted to be really open with him and tell him," she says, "I sat him down and said, 'I have something to tell you.' And he's like, 'What? What?' And I finally said, 'I'm a homosexual.' And he said, 'Is that all?' He really thought I was going to tell him something just horrible. Basically, his reaction was like: 'We were aware of this. We don't understand it, but as long as you're happy.' I was very, very lucky."

Her father died of cancer in 1991, and she dedicated her album *Never Enough* to him. "If you asked me before, what would hurt me the most, I would say losing my father," she says. "And that's just what happened. He was understanding and just everything you could ask for in a father."

I am amazed by her strength and talent.

—Chris Blackwell
ISLAND RECORDS

Stephen Herbits

CORPORATE EXECUTIVE

I really believe that the most important thing that any of us can do, for ourselves and for the rest of us; is to come out. The time is right in the business world; the emphasis is on diversity, and if a company is really serious about diversity, then it ought to include lesbians and gays. Given the growing recognition by American business of its competition in the world and the impact of productivity in the U.S. work-force, they're going to need us.

Steve is like a reincarnation of one of those Hindu gods with eight hands —one hand to hold his portable telephone, two hands to pound out policy papers, one to meet and greet those who can implement those policies, two to nudge the recalcitrant, and another two to embrace his friends.

—James Pepper
PHILANTHROPIST

As a high-ranking executive with Joseph E. Seagram & Sons, Stephen Herbits is forging an enviable path—not only because of his professional achievements, but also because he is succeeding as an openly gay man with an activist conscience.

Herbits didn't come out when he first joined Seagram in 1977. In the very early eighties, though, he learned that the son of one of Seagram's senior executives had AIDS. "I started talking to him about his gay son, and AIDS," says Herbits. "I made it very clear that I was gay. So it was in that context that I sort of made it official. I was reaching out to him, so I felt comfortable. Seagram is a pretty unusual place. I don't know of anyone who enjoys the kind of support and positive atmosphere in corporate America that I do."

Coming out also had tangible positive results on the job, where he deals with world-wide government relations, and political and policy issues. "My productivity is three or four times the level that it was before I was out, and I was a hard worker then. The experience of living a lie expends a lot of energy. Once you come out of the closet, that energy can be used for something more productive."

But coming out was just the beginning. After meeting an AIDS and gay rights activist in 1985, Herbits was spurred to help the fight against the epidemic. He became a founding board member of the National Leadership Coalition on AIDS and has also served on the boards of Gay Men's Health Crisis and chaired the AIDS Action Council. He also recently devoted his organizational and fundraising skills to the issue of gays in the military. He was well-connected to play a role; earlier in his career he had served as a special assistant to the Secretary of Defense, and later helped with the Defense Department transitions for the incoming Reagan and Bush Administrations. His defense work was part of eleven years of government service in Washington, including positions in the White House, on Capitol Hill, and in the trade representative's office.

His disappointment with the outcome of the campaign to end the ban doesn't put a damper on his enthusiasm for coming out, or the positive effect it can have on every facet of life. "The more we demand that institutions allow us to be who we are, the more they're going to have to."

Photographed by David Morgan

Carmen Vazquez

FEMINIST

I became an activist to reconcile myself, to give voice to experiences of oppression, and to resist the slow death of silence and inaction. At the core of my public message and organizing strategies as a lesbian and gay rights activist are three principles: working to end racism, individual autonomy in human sexuality, and economic justice.

In 1980 Carmen Vazquez, the founding director of the San Francisco Women's Building, was working with a group of women to keep the center open. Created through the combined efforts of the San Francisco Women's Center and the Bay Area women's community, the Women's Building was the first and is still the only women-owned-and-operated community center in the country. However, 1980 was a year marked by fear. The building had suffered an arsonist's fire, two bomb threats, and one actual bombing.

Many believed it was better to keep silent about those events. But Vazquez moved community members out of the paralyzing constraints of their fear by organizing a community meeting to discuss the threats and the future of the Women's Building. In her speech, Vazquez made clear the links between racial, economic, sexual, and gender based violence, dedicating the work of the Women's Building to all who have "suffered that violence which is a deprivation of rights." The speech also provided Vazquez with the context, outline, and direction of her work for the years to come.

A self-described "butch socialist," Vazquez shares her home in Berkeley, California with Marcia Gallo, her lover and life partner of ten years. In May 1991–eleven years after she was hired as its first director—the San Francisco Women's Building honored Vazquez for her work in establishing the building, strengthening the Bay Area lesbian movement, as well as her many achievements and contributions to improving the lives of lesbians and gay men, particularly those who are working class and of color.

Carmen brings a passionate spirit, and a clarity of purpose and vision to her work. She is an ally, in the strongest sense and tradition of that word, and I am proud to call her my friend.

—Sabrina Sojourner
WRITER

58

Photographed by Marc Geller

Eric Marcus

WRITER

Stepping into other people's lives is fascinating—you get into their heads, like a Vulcan mind meld. What I know how to do is draw people out about very private things in their lives, sometimes very painful things. My ability to do that has everything to do with the painful experiences in my own life. It would be very hard, in fact impossible, for me to do this work if I hadn't had my own misery.

When Eric Marcus was twelve years old his father committed suicide. He was an ex-Communist, a New York Jewish liberal, and a distinguished writer, who believed in the value of words. His death is at the root of much of what his son would become, as he grew up striving to emulate his father's intellectual nature, while being deeply affected by losing him. These contrasts would forge Marcus' voice as a writer.

Nowhere is that voice more evident than in the splendid and astute *Making History: The Struggle for Gay and Lesbian Equal Rights,* a massive work consisting of forty-nine interviews with people who had been involved with advancing the gay political and social effort in America, and were willing to share their impressions and personal histories. Marcus used his own voice to shape the real-life voices of his characters, and was able to make his subjects trust him. Judged the best non-fiction gay book of 1993 by the American Library Association and nominated for a Lambda Literary Award, the book became a national gay best-seller.

In a field driven by personal bitterness, stupid ideological disputes and the sound of grinding axes, Eric Marcus' educated neutrality is water in the desert.

—Matthew Paris
NATIONAL REVIEW

Underscoring much of *Making History's* honesty is Marcus' own struggle for self-acceptance. "I had terrible conflicts about being gay because it was such a *bad* thing," he says, "but when I was seventeen, I met Bob. He was sweet, sensitive, and sexy. He encouraged me to read about gay issues and to meet other gay kids. I fell in love with him and he fled, but I'm grateful for his gentleness." Marcus is committed to exploring what it feels like to be a gay or lesbian person in our society; his other books include *The Male Couple's Guide to Living Together; Is it a Choice? Answers to 300 of the Most Frequently Asked Questions About Gays and Lesbians;* and the witty and pessimistic *Expect the Worst (You Won't Be Disappointed).*

Currently working with Olympic diving champion Greg Louganis on his upcoming autobiography, Marcus is thoughtfully optimistic about his place in the world. He is touched by the love he feels from his family, particularly his mother, who is the New York media co-chair for Parents and Friends of Lesbians and Gays. "Sometimes I think my mother is more gay than I am," he says with a laugh. "Even though she isn't gay. No one could ask for a more supportive parent as an adult. And we all need that kind of support, don't you think?"

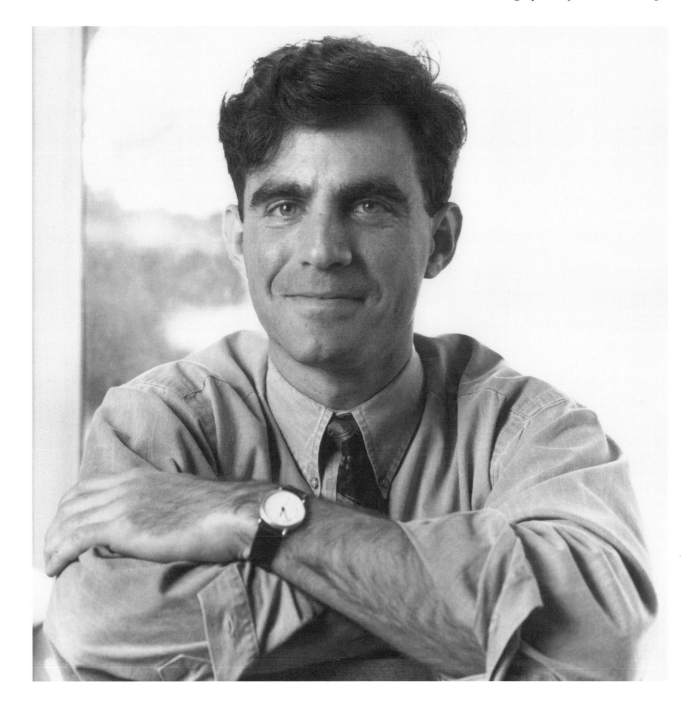

Photographed by JEB (Joan E. Biren)

Written by Karen Sundquist

Del Martin and Phyllis Lyon

LESBIAN RIGHTS PIONEERS

We were appalled when we heard people talking about having 'burnout.' What keeps us going is that we've been having fun—and we like a good challenge!

In 1953, three years after meeting in Seattle, Phyllis Lyon and Del Martin moved in together in San Francisco. They felt isolated and found no real community of lesbians outside of the lesbian bars, where women seemed to be in cliques, and Lyon and Martin were too shy to approach them. Eventually, through a gay male friend, they were introduced to another lesbian. That contact changed their lives, and in 1955, Lyon, Martin and six other women, founded the Daughters of Bilitis, a revolutionary organization named for Bilitis, a fictional woman who was said to have lived in Lesbos during the time of Sappho.

Through its regular meetings and its newsletter *The Ladder,* DOB membership increased and new chapters formed in cities across America. Much to their surprise, Martin and Lyon found themselves at the forefront of a newly emerging lesbian movement, and believe they were simply in the right place at the right time. "A straight friend once asked us, 'What are you doing this for?' " says Lyon. "We finally had to admit that we were doing it for ourselves, so we would have a place to dance together, and so that lesbians who were growing up wouldn't have to go through what we went through."

The couple organized the very first national DOB convention in 1960. "It was the first truly public lesbian event," remembers Martin. With more than two hundred participants, it was the largest gathering of any homophile organization up to that time. "Even the homosexual detail of the vice squad showed up!" says Lyon. "But our biggest problem was getting professionals to come and speak," says Martin. "Especially women, who were afraid of being branded as lesbians." And at a time when even the word "homosexual" didn't easily roll off the tongue, they published *Lesbian/Woman* and told how they came out, how they met and how they formed their partnership. For lesbians who came out in the 1970s, *Lesbian/Woman* was often the first affirming thing they read about being a lesbian.

After more than forty years as partners and warriors, Martin and Lyon show no signs of slowing down. They still do the work that they find most personal and closest to their hearts, which these days is doing outreach to elderly gay men and lesbians. The nineties have taken them to a new level where at long last they see articulate, committed leaders emerging among lesbian, gay, and bisexual youth. They are thrilled and delighted to watch this new era unfold, knowing all the while what each step of the journey was like—because they were there.

Lyon and Martin remove the mystification and the fears concerning lesbians.

—Benjamin Spock
AUTHOR AND PHYSICIAN

Mandy Carter

ACTIVIST

People were hung from trees for being Black. Today, people are beaten up and murdered for being gay and lesbian. Any Black person who can't equate being gay with being Black is essentially denying that gay and lesbian Black people exist.

We are proud of Mandy Carter and her work, and are happy to forge this partnership with the Black Gay and Lesbian Leadership Forum in order to enlist the support and goodwill of African-Americans to oppose the efforts of the radical right to institutionalize discrimination against gay and lesbian people. She is just the right leader for this struggle.

—Tim McFeeley
HUMAN RIGHTS
CAMPAIGN FUND

Mandy Carter is no neophyte to activism. During the anti-war movement, she relocated to Durham, North Carolina, where she eventually became campaign director of North Carolina Senate Vote '90, a political group initiated by gays and lesbians to unseat Senator Jessie Helms. She created a broad coalition of gay men and lesbians, women, environmentalists, artists, and many others who had first-hand experience with Helms' right-wing politics. During the campaign Carter was horrified that James Meredith, the first Black student to integrate the University of Mississippi, was on Helms' staff. After Helms narrowly won re-election, Carter heard about a white gay man who viewed Helms as the enemy, but couldn't bring himself to vote for Gantt because Gantt is Black. "I was just blown away," says Carter. "Maybe that's why the vote was so close."

Carter doesn't blindly point a finger just at white people. Ambivalence in the African-American community toward the lesbian and gay civil rights movement has been around for years. Bayard Rustin, the main architect for the 1963 March on Washington, was a Black, gay man. It was his work and vision that helped set the stage for Martin Luther King, Jr. to deliver his famous "I Have A Dream" speech. But because of his sexual identity, Rustin was denied recognition, and it wasn't until 1993 that Coretta Scott King and Jessie Jackson publicly acknowledged him. But they did acknowledge him. And Carter believes that the Black community and its churches are the new battleground for the gay, lesbian, and bisexual rights movement. To that end, Carter, a public policy advocate at the Human Rights Campaign Fund, in collaboration with the National Black Gay and Lesbian Leadership Forum, is directing the Fight The Right campaign. She is organizing in African-American communities where Pat Robertson's Christian Coalition and other predominately white radical religious groups have targeted the Black community with anti-gay ballot initiatives.

Yet organizing isn't enough if there isn't the money to back up the grassroots effort. "In 1993 the HRCF sent me to Cincinnati to help fight an anti-gay ballot initiative in Ohio," says Carter. "Colorado for Family Values poured four hundred thousand dollars into their campaign. They outspent us at Equality in Cincinnati nearly ten to one. They got one minister to be the "official" Black voice of faith. He spoke out against 'the wealthy, white gay men who want special rights.' Well, guess what. We lost."

Marvin Liebman

FOUNDER OF THE NATIONAL COALITION FOR UNDERSTANDING

The cement that held the conservative movement together was anti-communism. With the collapse of communism, the movement needed a new enemy to bond its disparate groups together. Homosexuals! It began with Mapplethorpe and the NEA. It was clear to me that the issue had little to do with art, obscene or otherwise. It had to do with utilizing bigotry, hatred, ignorance, and fear against lesbians and gay men to replace the unifying hatred of communism, and so to fuel 'conservative' fundraising operations. When I saw what was happening to the movement of which I had been an integral part, I knew what I had to do. I came out publicly in the pages of National Review (and The Advocate) as an openly gay man. I was sixty-seven years old.

Starting as an anti-Communist activist in the early 1950s, Marvin Liebman was a powerful force in the American conservative community, working closely for over thirty years with William F. Buckley, Jr., and the other leaders of the growing conservative movement. He organized Young Americans for Freedom, the American Conservative Union, and more than thirty-five other organizations and ad hoc committees. A master of agit-prop, he helped launch Barry Goldwater's campaign, Ronald Reagan's first try for the Presidency in 1968, and many other political campaigns in the 50s, 60s, and 70s. "During all those heady years I thought I was an open and free man," says Liebman. "But I was a deeply repressed person, cowering in the closet, keeping the fact that I am gay from the world. Articulating it was the most important, difficult and totally liberating action I have ever taken. Now I have a family that is truly my own—my gay and lesbian children and grandchildren—and I am able to live a full and normal life."

Liebman has recently founded the National Coalition for Understanding (NCU) in order to dispel the stereotypes of homosexuals. Although once embarrassed by the gay "sub-culture," Liebman now says, "It's *our* sub-culture. The Dykes on Bikes and the drag queens are fabulous. But to many people in the closet, they are terrifying. It is vital to our future for as many lesbians and gay men as possible to come out. It is equally vital to show them—and the American people—the entire face of our community, and not just the stereotypes of the Sisters of Perpetual Indulgence and pierced-nipple lesbians. I hope the NCU will help. That's what I'm trying to do."

Marvin was dealt a raw deal at birth. It would have been much easier had he been born a liberal. He is caught between the rock of ideology and the hard place of biology. His political affinities run toward people who denounce him as a homosexual. He has faced this situation with great good humor, and not a little courage.

—Ron Reagan
JOURNALIST

John J. McNeill

SPIRITUAL LEADER

The Vatican authorities gave me an order of silence that went beyond anything I could obey in good conscience. My ultimate obedience is to God and to discontinue my ministry would be to violate His will for me. God does not despise anything that God has created.

John McNeill exemplifies the best of what a Roman Catholic priest should be. He will go down in history for coming out, for speaking the truth about the gay and lesbian community, and for refusing to bow to the pressures of even the Pope in his quest to see justice done to all of God's children.

—Reverend Troy Perry
FOUNDER OF METROPOLITAN COMMUNITY CHURCHES

Father John J. McNeill was expelled from the Society of Jesus in 1987 after forty years of devotion to ministerial and teaching duties, and eventually lost the legal right to exercise his priesthood. Yet in spite of a demeaning series of Vatican-sanctioned rejections imposed upon him by the Jesuits, his beloved peers, he still considers his order, "one of the greatest groups of men on Earth."

McNeill helped found Dignity, a nationwide fellowship of lesbian, bisexual and gay Roman Catholics, and came out publicly on the *Today Show* in 1976, upon publication of his first book, *The Church and the Homosexual.* The Vatican immediately relieved him of his teaching duties which, in an ironic turn of the miter, freed him to direct his efforts toward a new career as a psychotherapist while continuing to minister to lesbian and gay Christians. But then came his expulsion. "I realized through these challenges," he says, "that the very process by which we free ourselves to accept our sexuality frees all of us to accept our true selves."

His efforts have increasingly focused on changing the teachings of the Catholic Church through his writings. His other books include *Taking a Chance on God* and his latest work, *Freedom, Glorious Freedom,* which is about the need for spiritual autonomy. "We must free ourselves from our dependence on all outside homophobic authority," he says. "Through our own feelings we learn what God wants for us." McNeill also conducts spiritual workshops and retreats, supporting the unique gifts and abilities embodied by lesbian and gay messengers of God's word.

McNeill calls for a rejection of all narrow interpretations of scripture imposed on the lesbian and gay community by outsiders with their own agenda, and casual conversation with him is sprinkled with tender deference to one of his personal heroes, St. Bernard of Clairvaux, who taught that, "We drink from our own wells." McNeill is a pragmatic spiritual scientist and weaver of ancient lore. "I believe as St. Ignatius Loyola," he says. "God is in continuous personal dialogue with those who seek the divine presence. He speaks to us principally not through the mind, but through the feelings." McNeill's call to God is an equal call to arms, and his teachings provide ammunition everyone can equally afford to bear.

Suzanne Westenhoefer

COMEDIAN
I like straight people. I just don't want them teaching our kids!

Never having appeared before as a comedian, Suzanne Westenhoefer entered a contest in 1990 at Kelly's Piano Bar in New York City. Whatever nerves she had disappeared when she was on-stage doing her three minutes, and she won the competition hands down. Since then she's had to get used to rave reviews, performing all over the country, and having her own HBO special. That's all right though. Some of her straight audiences have had to get used to something too: the fact that she is a happily out lesbian.

Westenhoefer challenges stereotypes and breaks down barriers. Audiences can only laugh and be part of the conspiracy to change our world into a more tolerant place. She's a comic whose timing and personality have made her one of the most exciting new faces on the scene today—a standout because she is a natural. "It's unfamiliarity and ignorance that breed contempt toward gay people," says Westenhoefer. "Through comedy, I believe I can make a difference."

Not one to limit her humor or her politics to the comedy stage, Westenhoefer also teaches young people about diversity. She is a popular speaker in high school classes where she discusses what it is like to be a lesbian. During the often-heated question and answer periods that follow her remarks, she challenges the students' attitudes about gay men and lesbians and makes them stop and think—about real life, love, and the freedom to be who you are. "They are generally very homophobic," she says. "Being kids, anything different is bad, but there is also always one in each class who really lights up. It's the most important thing I do, even more than when I do comedy."

She's a center stage Diva who bursts out of her closet with little explosions of outspoken bemusement that could make even Bette Midler blush.

—Michael Musto
NEW YORK DAILY NEWS

Photographed by Glenn Jessen
Courtesy Olivia Records

Dave Kopay

FORMER PROFESSIONAL FOOTBALL PLAYER
Hey, I'm not the only one!

Nearly two decades ago, in December of 1975, pro football running back Dave Kopay, a ten year NFL veteran who was playing for the Washington Redskins, picked up a copy of the *Washington Star.* The headline said, "Homosexuals in Sports/Why Gay Athletes Have Everything to Lose." Kopay says, "I could not believe I was reading those words." In a series of articles, over sixty players, coaches and psychologists were interviewed. Of the group, not one gay athlete agreed to let his or her name be used; but the love that dared not speak its name was yelling for attention, and on the sports page no less. In his 1977 autobiography, Kopay remembers how, reading that article, he "sat there choking back laughter and tears." A man who had spent his entire adult life feeling confused, isolated and ashamed, was seeing that his secret was not just "me," it was "us."

But soon Kopay became angry. He felt that somebody had to talk—had to put a name to those articles about gay athletes. He went to the writer and editor of the series and offered to come out, but they tried to talk him out of it. As the headline said, he had everything to lose. But sometimes Kopay likes to jump without a net, and though he knew things could, and probably would, go badly for him, he decided to tell the truth. It made international headlines. America wasn't used to seeing gay people in the press then, much less in the form of a respected, macho sports professional. A new prototype was created, of a butch, brawny athlete who happens to be gay—portrayed successfully by former pro football players Bob Seagren in the television series *Soap* and Alex Karras in the film *Victor/Victoria.*

Kopay is still talking—in occasional interviews and public appearances. Though he works as a sales manager in his uncle's floorcovering business in Los Angeles, he has no trouble fitting the occasional *Donahue* or *Geraldo* appearance into his schedule, and at fifty-one still pumps iron regularly in the gym after work. Although he used to define men by their masculinity, Kopay has learned a bit about the full spectrum of homosexuals, and is no longer scared to be with, or be seen with, those who are not like himself. "I think my life is much more interesting now," he says, "and a lot more fun. I can laugh a lot more, and at the same time still be taken seriously when I need to be. I think that's important too."

I know there are guys who would love to play against Dave Kopay and break his neck for how he 'tainted their image.' But I respect Dave very much for what he did.

—Ben Davidson
FORMER
OAKLAND RAIDER

72

Photograph Courtesy Hetrick-Martin Institute

Written by Adriene Corbin

Damien Martin and Emery S. Hetrick

FOUNDERS OF THE HETRICK-MARTIN INSTITUTE

We should not be ashamed of standing up for the most vulnerable in our community—our youth. We'll never have a healthy adult community unless we reach them when they're young. This must become a part of the movement, not just for gay and lesbian kids, but also for the ninety percent who are not gay, who must learn not to hate.

A gay boy living in a Manhattan home for runaway teens had just been attacked while showering and gang-raped by several heterosexual boys who were also living in the facility. The staff responded by turning the gay teenager back onto the street while his rapists remained sheltered. When they heard what had happened, Emery S. Hetrick and Damien Martin were enraged. That a youth advocacy agency could view the boy's homosexuality as the problem, rather than the sexual assault by his attackers—and the fact that this sort of discrimination and abuse was all too typical of what gay and lesbian youth experience—could no longer go unchallenged. "They knew it would take over their lives, and it did," says Andy Humm, a longtime colleague and friend of the couple. "But they also knew they had to do something for the kids. And they did it at a time when the personal and professional risks were tremendous. No one else was willing to take on the issue of gay youth for fear of being called a child molester."

Hetrick was a psychiatrist and professor at New York University Medical School, and Damien Martin was a communications professor at NYU. In 1979, shortly following the rape of that teenage boy, they founded the Institute for the Protection of Lesbian and Gay Youth, which would come to include the Harvey Milk School. Hetrick and Martin felt that the problems faced by homosexual youth do not stem from sexual orientation, but from society's stigmatization of homosexuals. They taught gays and lesbians the value of their self-worth. After Hetrick's death from AIDS in 1987, the agency was renamed the Hetrick-Martin Institute. It was and continues to be a national model for gay and lesbian youth advocacy agencies.

On the day of Emery Hetrick's funeral, the procession, including family members and human rights activists, arrived at the gateway of the cemetery. Martin went in to authorize the opening of the grave and was told that a family member's approval was required. His Irish temper roused to a pitch: "We loved one another for twelve years. We bought this plot together and soon I will be buried here beside him. You will open the grave and get him buried today!" Damien Martin died of AIDS four years later and was buried next to Hetrick. Together, their righteous indignation, love and courage created a legacy for gay and lesbian youth.

I won't forget those days when we planted flowers and trees while discussing how to best meet the needs of gay and lesbian youth. I realize now that among the flowers and trees were also planted the seeds of Damien and Emery's vision from which sprang their legacy.

—Joyce Hunter
NATIONAL LESBIAN AND
GAY HEALTH CARE
FOUNDATION

Frank Buttino

FORMER FBI SPECIAL AGENT

If I have to get up before the office in San Diego and say I'm homosexual, I can do that. If I've got to go to court and say I'm homosexual and I was an FBI agent, I may do that. I don't know. I'm not trying to threaten the Bureau, but someone has to have the courage to stand up and say, 'This is wrong. I'm homosexual and I'm a good agent.'

When Janet Reno announced at the end of 1993 that the Justice Department would no longer disqualify its employees solely on the basis of their sexual orientation, Frank Buttino heaved a deep sigh of satisfaction. The Attorney General's statement was precisely one of Buttino's goals in his lawsuit against his former employers. For twenty years he had worked for the Justice Department's most famous division, The Federal Bureau of Investigation.

Buttino was a model agent. For his San Diego-based investigations of narcotics and organized crime, he received steady commendations and a superior job performance rating. But when he was anonymously outed to his employers, Special Agent Buttino was first suspended, then fired. In between came a series of harrowing interrogations; at one polygraph preparation, his FBI interrogator told Buttino that if other agents had known he is gay, they would have killed him.

At the end of that day of questioning, Buttino's outrage surpassed the intimidation, and he found he had the courage to sue. By 1992 his case was expanded to a class action suit with more than three dozen co-plaintiffs, some extrapolated from the estimated one hundred people the policy had affected (one investigator told Buttino that the Bureau drummed out approximately one gay agent per week). Buttino published a book about his ordeal, *A Special Agent: Gay and Inside the FBI*, went on tour, and kept the spotlight on the FBI's biased policy.

In December of 1993, the FBI agreed not to discriminate against applicants or employees on the basis of sexual orientation or because of private, consensual homosexual conduct. They agreed to hire Dana Tillson, a lesbian applicant who testified at Buttino's trial. Lesbian and gay rights advocates expect the Buttino case to have a wide-reaching impact on the policy towards all federal employees, including those in the military. After a lifetime in the closet, Frank Buttino became something he never quite expected to be—a landmark gay activist.

Mr. Buttino makes an excellent appearance and I would rate him above-average. I think this agent has the potential for advancement in the service.

—J. Edgar Hoover
1972

76

Lorri L. Jean

ACTIVIST

When I came out, the lesbian outfit of choice was flannel shirts and blue jeans. If you had told me back then that running a queer organization would require me to attend banquets and get me wearing sequins and heels, I'd have thought you were from another planet. But I'm sure my mother is thrilled.

Lorri L. Jean is a political activist who defies standard definitions—tough enough to stand up to the CIA, and brave enough to enjoy (and defy) lesbian tradition: When she attended the Womyn's Music Festival in Hart, Michigan in 1990, she felt great kinship with the thousands of other spirited lesbians (both in and out of flannel shirts). Yet each evening, as many of the women returned to their tents on the dusty campsite and waited in line at outdoor shower stalls, Jean would retreat into a different sort of home away from home—she had a rented a modern R.V. with all the amenities, and had also brought along her mother. Jean wanted to experience the festival in style and in good company. Her mother had a fabulous time.

As the oldest in a "very functional" farm family, Jean was raised to believe in herself and act accordingly. Dishonesty was viewed as a cardinal sin, so Jean never felt compelled to hide her sexuality. When her job as associate general counsel for the Federal Emergency Management Agency required security clearance, Jean announced without hesitation that she is a lesbian. But this was a Republican Administration. No matter. Jean became the first openly gay or lesbian person to ever fight for, and win, security clearance from the CIA.

She has always fought for justice. Even as a law student at Georgetown, she was lead plaintiff in a winning suit that forced the Jesuit university to recognize gay and lesbian student groups on campus. Her community activism in Washington included serving as president of the Gay and Lesbian Activist Alliance, chair of the District of Columbia's Commission on Domestic Partnership, board member of Lambda Legal Defense and Education Fund, and as the coordinator of gay and lesbian sensitivity training at the D.C. police academy. When FEMA promoted Jean to deputy regional director and moved her to San Francisco, she became the highest ranking openly gay employee of the Reagan/Bush years.

Today Jean lives in Hollywood with her partner, Gina M. Calvelli. As head of the Los Angeles Gay and Lesbian Community Services Center, the world's largest gay and lesbian center, Jean continues to do what she does best—facing challenges and building coalitions. And she makes her mother proud!

One gets a feeling of strength from Lorri Jean, like she is in control without being controlling. She exudes confidence and I believe is an excellent spokesperson and role model for our movement.

—Deborah Johnson

NATIONAL GAY AND LESBIAN TASK FORCE

Gregg Araki

FILMMAKER

The younger generation doesn't care about political correctness. My own films are sort-of controversial because of their punk-rock attitude and negativism. Lots of mainstream gays hate them.

Wow, groovy, cool. The thin kid with the straight raven-like hair falling in his face stood at the back of the packed two thousand-seat theater in Locarno, Switzerland, watching the audience applaud his $5,000 black-and-white sixteen millimeter film *Three Bewildered People in the Night*. He felt as if in a dream, not because, "They like me, they like me," but more because, "They get me," says Araki about the film festival. "It was a totally surreal experience because this was something that I had only watched on my living room wall before, and I never showed it to my friends because I thought they'd reject it."

That was 1987. Five movies later, he is still noted as the intensely hip, off-beat bratty kid of the gay underground film world. He shirks the New Queer Cinema label foisted on him and thumbs his nose at Hollywood and the gay community. A wannabee Marvel Comics artist/filmmaker, Araki is something of a visual anarchist who remains immune to the high-pressure of agents and publicists despite the fact that his film budgets are at last increasing (he is now working on the $1 million *Nowhere,* his first movie with actual financial backing). Compared to Jean-Luc Goddard, Andy Warhol, Pedro Almodovar, John Waters, and Derek Jarman, Araki shrugs off the criticism, complaints, awards and accolades alike. "No critic knows my work better than me," he says. "My films are very self-indulgent in that they're exactly the films I want to make about what interests me."

The AIDS crisis sparked his erotic and crass $23,000 road movie *The Living End* which features two angry, HIV-positive men on an escapist rampage. The heroes have sex on a deserted beach while one of them holds a pistol in his mouth. Araki dedicated the film "to the hundreds of thousands who've died and the hundreds of thousands more who will die because of a big White House full of Republican fuckheads." Reading about a teen who drank Drano and drowned in the family pool because of his homosexual guilt prompted Araki to put six mixed-up teenagers in a free-associative narrative with the provocative title *Totally F***ked Up*. Savagely ironic—his spit-in-your-face free-wheeling style of filmmaking oozes sensuality. His work is explicit, shoestring and gay. "As far as I know," he says, "I will always be gay. That's a reflection of my personality and identity, not the only part, but a big part."

Araki's bold mixture of black, gross-out humor and frank homoeroticism isn't likely to please the Pat Buchanan crowd.

—NEWSWEEK

Rodger McFarlane and Tom Viola

DIRECTORS OF BROADWAY CARES/EQUITY FIGHTS AIDS

Rodger's greatest strength is that he is relentless in not avoiding conflict. —Tom Viola

Tom's the greatest field marshall you can imagine. Plus he has a real flair—for making me look good! —Rodger McFarlane

We can't say the words 'Broadway Cares/Equity Fights AIDS' at a benefit or theatre performance without saying the names of Tom Viola and Rodger McFarlane. They are the reasons we are there.

—Cameron Mackintosh
PRODUCER

Everyone seems to mistake Rodger McFarlane and Tom Viola for each other. Well, they do sort of look alike (okay—they are both bald, but McFarlane is the tall one), but while they work for the same cause, their styles couldn't be more different. McFarlane's brash, shoot-from-the-hip attitude has been perfected through his decade-long commitment to AIDS fundraising and advocacy as one of the founders of GMHC and ACT UP. Viola is a bit quieter, his real strength coming in a methodical approach to getting things done.

But they both know how to work a room. At a fundraiser or event, you'll see their one-two punch work to perfection. Watch McFarlane move in to make the pitch: a message that a song or an appeal from a celebrity can provide just the right spin to open the hearts and wallets of the theatre-going public. Viola follows him to close the deal. Seamless. "We make it safe for people to act out many things," says Viola. "In addition to the anger and grief, people have an opportunity to feel useful and find strength being in this together."

The generosity and spirit of the theatre community has raised millions for direct support of people with AIDS and contributions to other AIDS service providers across the country. Audiences at BC/EFA events are treated to the elaborately staged Easter Bonnet and Gypsy of the Year competitions, cabaret and concert performances, flea markets, county fairs—and even events like *Broadway Bares,* where Broadway's best bodies strip for cash. And that's just in New York. Across the country, grassroots collaboration reaches people who might never have responded—until a favorite country music or soap star actually says the word, "AIDS," or wears a red ribbon.

McFarlane and Viola have both had heroes in their lives. McFarlane names his mentor, ex-lover, and now friend Larry Kramer as an important influence. "He taught me the difference between talking and doing, that you have responsibilities," says McFarlane. Viola's former boss at Actors Equity Association, Colleen Dewhurst, "set the standard," he says. "I learned the effect that a person can have simply by sharing their basic humanity." These two giants gave them a vision far bigger than they would have imagined themselves.

Lesser humans might buckle. After all, it's one thing to volunteer for an organization; it's another to live and breathe a cause every day. But as Viola says, "It would be criminal for me to do anything else. I would have to be drunk and stoned all the time to do nothing." Uncharacteristically, McFarlane just nods, and says with a grin, "Ditto."

Katherine V. Forrest

NOVELIST

To me the great pride, the miracle really, is the gay and lesbian community. We're the only community that takes in all color and creed, all races. It is so important to me as a writer to try to convey that in my work, the diversity and the power of all these various elements.

Best-selling novelist and mystery writer Katherine V. Forrest came late to full-time writing, but has been making up for lost time. In the years since her first novel, the lesbian erotic classic *Curious Wine*, appeared in 1983, Forrest has published nine books and edited three anthologies. "Much of my aspiration as a writer," says Forrest, "comes out of the experience of my own life, because I know that if I'd had any sort of role model growing up, what a difference that would have made!" *Curious Wine* worked to fill a gap Forrest had long felt. "I hadn't read anything that conveyed the passion and the beauty of our love, of how very beautiful women are together," she says. "That was what I wanted to do in the book."

Writing lesbian mysteries featuring detective Kate Delafield gives Forrest another chance to explore issues close to her. "I write to entertain," she says. "I don't want to preach to anybody—I *hate* novels that preach—but I do want to raise the issues that are of concern to us." Using her highly popular series as a lens, Forrest has looked at everything from childhood sexual abuse to prostitution, gay bashing to internalized homophobia. "My whole object is to portray lesbian life in process," she says. "Kate Delafield is a woman in a high-visibility, high-pressure position who is a closeted lesbian. I like exploring how she deals with that."

When not working on her next novel, the San Francisco-based Forrest works on other women's books in her role as senior editor for Naiad Press. A helpful influence on more than one young author, she takes this work very seriously. "I'm hungry," she says, "just terribly hungry, still, for lesbian literature. There's no way we're going to have the writers we want unless we work with them and develop their talent." Winner of two Lambda Literary Awards, Forrest also feels a large sense of responsibility to her gay and lesbian readership. "If life does imitate art," she says, "I think perhaps our literature has impact out of all proportion. As writers we must always be very aware of that."

Forrest populates her novels with a wide range of characters that stretch well beyond racial, ethnic, class and lifestyle stereotypes. She deals squarely with ethical and political hot potatoes, enjoys an avid readership, and has earned it.

—SAN FRANCISCO CHRONICLE

Written by Daniel Jacobson

Cleve Jones

NAMES PROJECT FOUNDER

When I look back on everything that has happened in the gay movement since I was a teenager in 1972, I am amazed. I know a lot of people are impatient because we've suffered so many deaths and still have to fight for our basic rights. I myself am furious and depressed about it. But I still wake up every morning with a sense of astonishment at how far we've come.

Jones stepped down as head of the Names Project in 1989, but still travels around the country with the Quilt, bringing its dual message of healing and activism to the American heartland. His work is changing our culture's approach to AIDS.

—Randy Shilts
JOURNALIST

When the mile-long Rainbow Flag unfurls along Fifth Avenue on Lesbian and Gay Pride Day this year to the cheers of thousands, it will be because Cleve Jones had another bright idea. This would not surprise anyone who knows him. Jones, who founded the Names Project/AIDS Memorial Quilt in 1987, has been rallying the lesbian and gay community around bright ideas for years.

Early in his political life, Jones mastered the ability to turn ideas that motivate people into actions moving the lesbian and gay community forward. A leader of gay street rallies and protests in San Francisco in the 1970s, he was Harvey Milk's aide and was at Milk's side when the San Francisco supervisor was murdered by an assassin's bullet in 1978. Jones organized the candlelight procession that followed Milk's death and the massive community response when Milk's killer, Dan White, was convicted of voluntary manslaughter rather than first-degree murder, thanks to the now-infamous "Twinkie defense." Legislative appointments in the California State Assembly followed, and Jones was on a fast-track from street activism to insider politics as an advocate for lesbian and gay causes.

When AIDS hit the gay community in the early 1980s, Jones was instantly reactive to the health crisis. In 1982 he helped create the San Francisco AIDS Foundation, one of this country's first AIDS organizations. As he watched friends and lovers sicken and die, and eventually discovered he himself was HIV-positive, he turned to AIDS activism. In 1987 Jones led a national march on the White House, protesting the Reagan administration's inaction on AIDS. But protests and marches were not enough to help him and others come to terms with overwhelming grief and anxiety; so Jones stitched together a simple panel of three-foot by six-foot cloth in remembrance of his friend Marvin Feldman—the beginning of his effort to recruit support for a memorial quilt honoring all who had died of AIDS. Thus was the Names Project born. The Quilt now has more than twenty-six thousand panels and has raised over $1.3 million for AIDS-related causes. When it went on display in Washington, D.C. in 1992, it covered thirteen acres and received four hundred thousand visitors.

k.d. lang

SINGER/SONGWRITER

I love having a cryptic sexuality. I was always most intrigued by people who were mysterious in that aspect. Androgyny is a natural thing for me, but it's also that I don't want to sell my music through sexuality.

For years it was clear to all but the most willfully ignorant that k.d. lang is gay. Her stage shows always contained numerous teasing confessions: after a dramatic pause, she would sometimes say, "Yes, it's true...I'm, a L-L-Lawrence Welk fan!" She played a love scene with another woman in the movie *Salmonberries*, further tantalizing her already smoldering admirers. Yet she had been cautious about coming out officially in the press, and protective of her mother back in Canada. But at last she made matters relatively plain in an *Advocate* interview last year, exclaiming, "I want to be out!" It was that simple.

Yet lang has intimated that her path in life seems to force an inexorable loneliness upon her, and that her music must often occupy the place of a lover. The emotional storms unleashed by her extraordinary voice are the quintessence of yearning. When she sang *Cryin'* with the late Roy Orbison, it was so powerful that his widow asked her to perform it again at the 1989 Songwriter's Hall of Fame banquet. Mining the terrain of such idols as Patsy Cline (of whom lang occasionally declares herself the reincarnation), she might have been embraced by the country music establishment at the beginning of her career, but she didn't play by the rules. Instead, she cultivated her trademark short-haired, tailored look, campaigned for People for the Ethical Treatment of Animals, and generally flouted convention at every turn.

No matter. She is one of her generation's sharpest songwriters and arguably its finest interpreter of the great song standards. From her performance-arty roots in country pastiche to the sophisticated adult pop of her Grammy award-winning 1992 album *ingenue*, lang has won legions of fans with her phenomenally rich and versatile voice and her powerful stage presence. Watch her sometime. Listen. Even her silences can break your heart.

You have to resist the emotional force of the music to analyze its eclectic inspiration, and that's not so easy to do when she has you wrapped around her little finger.

—Linda Kohanoo

PULSE

David B. Mixner

POLITICAL CONSULTANT

It's always sort of amazing to me that people think gays and lesbians not wanting to lose their jobs because of who they are, is 'special treatment.' Not wanting to walk down the street in fear that some- one will jump out of a pick-up with a baseball bat, is 'special treatment.' Being able to live with the one you love, is 'special treatment.' No one is talking about quotas or affirmative actions. We are talk- ing about the Constitution. That's all.

Put David B. Mixner's scrapbook next to Bill Clinton's. As you leaf through their respective memorabilia, you will see a lot of similarities—more than just their shared interest in politics or their respective histories of academic excellence. There are very specific parallels; records of each of them at the same marches, photos of their meeting twenty-five years ago at a reunion of the McCarthy-Kennedy coalition, documents of their shared time at Oxford. You can't help wonder why the tables aren't turned. Why isn't Clinton the friend and adviser to Mixner, the President?

Certainly one answer to that question is that Mixner is gay. But you have to go back to 1977, when he first came out, to understand what that means. It was a very different time. Though the drumbeats of the gay civil rights movement were pounding, gays were still "fags" to most people. For Mixner, a young man with political aspirations, coming out could have jeopardized everything. "I was lying so much about who I was, and where I was, and who my partners were," he says. "Even I would lose track of what the truth was. Coming out made me a free man. There's no substitute for freedom. Ever." Mixner seized his new freedom, becoming a pioneer in the political process for gay and lesbian people—a role that took a dramatic turn when Clinton ran for the presidency. As a member of Clinton's kitchen cabinet during the campaign, Mixner was able to bring gay and lesbian issues to the national agenda, and to mobilize the community behind Clinton. "It was a heady, hopeful time for us," says Mixner, "which we desperately needed after twelve years of darkness."

Yet all too soon, Mixner was faced with a dilemma that tested his convictions and principles. He would oppose Clinton's handling of the ban on gays in the military. He could risk his friendship and access to the President, or remain quiet. Mixner came out forcefully against the policy, even getting arrested in front of the White House at a demonstration—and still remains an unofficial advisor to the President. Mixner believes that Clinton's election forever changed history. "Is he the solution to all of our problems? No. We are," he says. "But never in our history have we had anyone come so close to being such a friend to this community. Yet now is not the time for rest, because our work is just beginning."

If there is one person responsible for bringing our movement to the point of being a major force, it's David Mixner. He is our visionary.

—Judge Steve Lachs

LOS ANGELES SUPERIOR COURT

Written by Simon Glickman

David Geffen

ENTERTAINMENT INDUSTRY EXECUTIVE AND AIDS ACTIVIST

We've shown America that we are no longer afraid of ourselves or ashamed of ourselves. We have had the courage in the face of an unprecedented onslaught to reach out to each other and show the country the true meaning of family values.

As David Geffen stood before the huge audience in the Universal Amphitheater to receive AIDS Project Los Angeles' Commitment to life Award in November 1992, he noted the loss of many friends and colleagues; "When the first person I knew died, I could not throw away his Rolodex card. So I saved it. I now have a rubber band around three hundred forty-one cards."

Geffen's appearance at the awards ceremony had begun with four words echoing through the auditorium: "As a gay man," he had said, "I have come a long way to be here tonight." *As a gay man.* Geffen had long used his considerable influence and visibility in the fight against AIDS, but coming out in an industry that treasures secrets and often shuns public vulnerability was an act of rare courage.

The story of Geffen's rise in the entertainment industry is well known—the son of Russian immigrants who started in the William Morris mail room and became the music industry phenomenon behind the Eagles, Linda Ronstadt, Guns N'Roses and Nirvana; the hit film producer successfully ventured onto Broadway with *Dreamgirls, M. Butterfly, Cats* and *Miss Saigon*; the Hollywood billionaire who dines with the President and advises on policy. But by coming out, he accomplished something altogether different. He showed a generation of lesbians and gay men that there is no limit to what they might achieve—he turned on its head the stereotype of what it means to be gay.

Geffen remains intensely committed to the fight against AIDS, and has donated several million dollars to various AIDS causes, including a $1 million check to APLA and another $1 million check to the Gay Men's Health Crisis in New York. He is outspoken in his attempts to turn political rhetoric into government action. "My power is the ability to believe in things, and to stick to them, and not take no for an answer," he said in a recent *BAM* interview. "Power isn't your ability to push people around; that's bad karma. And it always comes back and kicks you in the ass. I've been doing this for a very, very long time, and have been successful for twenty-something-odd years. So my karma must be pretty good."

Geffen is the stuff industry legends are made of.

- LOS ANGELES TIMES

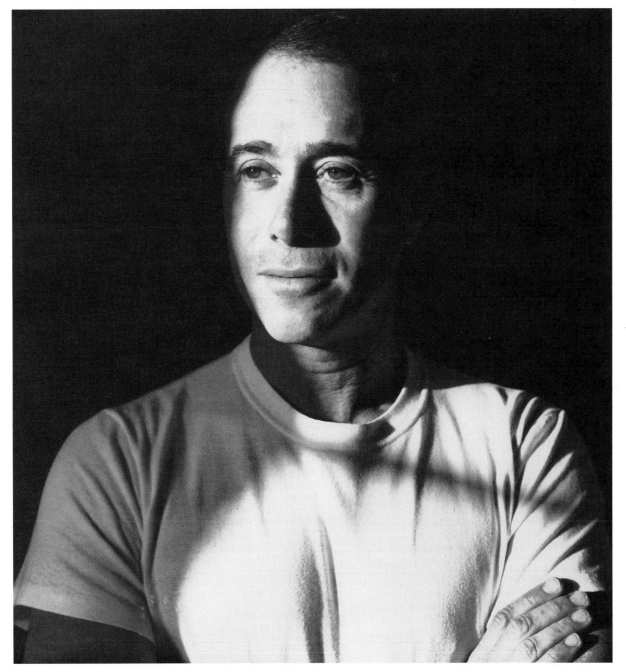

Terry Sweeney

ACTOR AND WRITER

I don't want to be butch or straight, just what I am. I'm a shaman, a jester. My most important role is the one in which I hold up a mirror to society and reflect what is there.

The first openly gay comic on network television was the tall, unique looking, genuinely funny Terry Sweeney. He was hired for the 1986-87 season of *Saturday Night Live* by producers who were not as brave as they had convinced themselves they were. It was a year of strain for this gifted actor, who kept standing up for himself, trying to get an entrenched corporate mentality to push past its fears and stereotyped ideas of what "gay" meant. Although he ended up being placed on the television equivalent of the sports-bench, he did develop a series of memorable satirical portraits: Patti LaBelle, Joan Collins, and his best-known achievement, Nancy Reagan. He even played the First Lady with First Son, Ron Reagan, the week he hosted.

Sweeney enjoyed great success with a national tour of his Nancy Reagan show, *It's Still My Turn*, including a six-month stint in Manhattan, and most importantly, he found happiness. "A house, a husband and a dog," he said in a *People* interview. "I have everything I ever wanted." He also turned to screenwriting, and has had two features produced, *Love At Stake* in 1988, and *Shag* in 1989, written with Lanier Laney (the husband referred to in *People*), his partner since 1982.

Beneath his banter and quick wit lies a serious mind striving to understand homophobia, both in the straight community and deep within the gay and lesbian community itself. To that end, he has stopped accepting gay roles that don't encompass the full spectrum of being gay. "I've gotten tired of the mean-queen syndrome, those Priss-Pots who live alone and are cool and hardened," he says. "I've turned down roles which are homophobic and hateful, and I've called up the casting directors and bitched to them about it." As an alternative to the stereotypes usually seen in the media, Sweeney is busily pitching a television series that would feature a gay couple.

Sweeney is a pioneer and he accepts it. "When you're in those covered wagons on broken roads, the ones who are following don't know all the hardship needed to tame that new ground," he says. "Internalized homophobia hurts gay actors, so if you're a gay actor, go find fellow champions—non-gay as well as gay—who are courageous, and look to work with them. The industry will change for gays just as it's changed for racial minorities and women. Look at me. Being openly gay, I still work. So can you."

He's a unique talent who deserves to be seen and heard. We need him in Hollywood.

—Penny Marshall
DIRECTOR AND ACTRESS

Photographed by Ron Reagan

Mica England

ACTIVIST

We must begin to stop the hatred within our own spheres of influence. Hatred and negativity will cause our destruction.

Standing before the Dallas City Council in July 1989 as they considered a resolution in support of the students in China fighting for democracy, Mica England held up an equal employment opportunity poster and demanded justice: "I responded to an advertisement for Dallas police officers in the *Tulsa Oklahoma World*. Before the recruiters invited me to Dallas to take the examination, I told them I am gay," England said to the Council. "But when I arrived they refused to let me take the test because I openly and willingly admitted that I am gay. Why is there no democracy for *me* in Dallas?"

England's pointed remarks totally disrupted the meeting. One council member demanded the city attorney provide legal basis for the police department's exclusionary ban, and the mayor tried to save face by hastily adjourning the meeting. Another council member asked, "Is this resolution in support of all Chinese students or only the heterosexual ones?" In the uproar, one thing was clear: the Council had no intention of dealing with the issue publicly. But England sued in 1990, and the Council was forced to hold a public hearing in January 1992. Lasting until 2:30 a.m. with six hundred people in attendance, the meeting was angry and emotionally charged. Conservative and religious groups put homophobic slogans and banners all around the room, even placing *No Homo Cops* badges on infants.

The Council voted to continue the hiring ban on gays and lesbians. But weeks after the hearing, England won her lawsuit. The court ruled that the rationale for refusing to hire gay and lesbian officers (the Texas homosexual sodomy law) was unconstitutional, and ordered the Dallas Police Department to allow England to apply for a position. It was a much larger victory than anyone had anticipated. When five gay and lesbian Texans later sued successfully to overturn the state's homosexual sodomy law, the Texas Supreme Court refused to hear the state's appeal, citing England's case as precedent.

Mica England had one desire: she had wanted to be a police officer. Although she used her hard-won legal victory, and applied for a position on the force, she later realized the court case had made her too famous, and her effectiveness would be compromised. Sadly, she abandoned the dream that had set her on her trail-blazing path. But in her single-minded determination to reach a personal goal, England had made Texas history. That's no small thing.

I am very impressed with Mica. She's a real fighter and I'm glad she won her case.

—Larry King
LARRY KING LIVE

Barbara Grier and Donna McBride

PUBLISHERS

What we look forward to is the day when any young woman, anywhere in the world, can wake up and say "I'm a lesbian,' and then go to the corner bookstore and find a book that will tell her, 'Yes, indeed you are. And you're wonderful.'

The reigning co-queens of lesbian publishing, Barbara Grier and Donna McBride, partners in both love and business, started working on evenings and weekends twenty-one years ago, and they built a business together. Naiad Press, the result of their hard work, is now the world's oldest and largest lesbian publishing house, a $1.6 million business with over two hundred fifty books published and twenty-four new titles appearing annually. "What I'm proudest of," says McBride, "is that we are doing something important for the movement and we're doing it in a way that allows us to make a living out of it—and even provide a living for other women too."

When Grier talks of her accomplishments, the first thing she mentions is not Naiad or her sixteen years as a writer, and later as an editor, on *The Ladder,* an early lesbian magazine. Instead she speaks of the couple's personal library of gay and lesbian books, periodicals and photos that they donated to the Gay and Lesbian Center of the San Francisco Public Library, slated for completion in 1995. "I'm prouder of that than of almost anything," she says of the massive collection she started in her late teens. "That stuff will be around a hundred years after I'm gone."

Both women are in agreement about the importance of publishing affirmative lesbian novels. "The things that are destructive to us," says Grier, "are the closet and a lack of pride, which comes from internalized homophobia. Virtually all of our problems will be solved by coming out and standing tall."

By proving the viability of publishing lesbian fiction, Barbara Grier and Donna McBride have inspired a whole generation of feminist and small presses that publish lesbian work. But by also demonstrating the profitability of lesbian fiction, Naiad Press has changed mainstream publishing's willingness to publish lesbian fiction, hopefully forever.

—Carol Seejay
FEMINIST BOOKSTORE NEWS

Photographed by JEB (Joan E. Biren)

David Morgan

PHOTOGRAPHER

It's important that young gay people see positive images of themselves as romantic figures, in relationships, and showing great passion for each other.

When a bar on Manhattan's Upper West Side hung an exhibit of David Morgan's photographs of male nudes in May 1992, he didn't take it all that seriously. "These photos were taken for sexy disco invitations and meant to be instantly disposable," says Morgan. "I jokingly called myself 'the reigning king of refrigerator art.' " However, seeing the images displayed together for the first time, the photographer gained a new appreciation of his own work. "I felt that perhaps I was an artist," he says, "and not simply providing a service like plumbing."

Morgan moved to New York from Eugene, Oregon to become an actor. He immediately embarked upon a successful theatrical career, playing leading roles in national tours of Broadway musicals. With an amateur's flair for photography, he began taking head shots of his fellow actors. Their agents, impressed with his work, recommended him to their other clients, and an effective sideline business was born. Eventually, Morgan's late lover, Michael, became tired of Morgan's constant touring. "Show business had become about not staying home," says Morgan. "Then when my father died and I needed to support my mother, I made a painful decision to focus on my photography and phase out my acting career."

When his 1990 photograph announcing the Saint's annual White Party became an indelible image of joyous gay communal sexuality taped to countless refrigerators throughout New York, Morgan began to realize what an impact a photograph could have. "That photo of seven men in their underwear affectionately grabbing each other certainly struck a chord in a lot of people," he says. Morgan's photography provides us with a post-AIDS romantic view of sex. He stays away from the S&M-inspired imagery of the early eighties and creates a sweet world of muscular gym buddies tumbling out of clean, white shorts.

"In the beginning, my models were bankers, brokers, doctors, professional people who didn't want their faces shown in a nude photograph. This limitation became something of an artistic trademark," he says. "By keeping their faces in shadow, I was actually making the images more universal. They now became all of us." What began as disposable club advertising has developed into a body of work—reproduced on greeting cards, calendars and purchased as works of art. "I like to think that my photographs are about more than merely a torso," he says. "That perhaps they tell a story about an intimate relationship. In a way, it's theater."

David Morgan's imagery challenges society's assumption that gay men and women are merely sexual deviants. Most straights find his images of tenderness and affection between men to be far more threatening, if not perverse, than anything Robert Mapplethorpe presented to us in the 1980s.

—Frank Gerlando
ART FORMS GALLERY

Harvey Milk

SAN FRANCISCO BOARD OF SUPERVISORS

Every gay person must come out. As difficult as it is, you must tell your immediate family and your relatives. You must tell your friends, if indeed they are your friends. You must tell your neighbors. You must tell the people you work with. Once they realize we are indeed their children, we are indeed every-where, every myth, every lie, every innuendo will be destroyed once and for all. And once—once you do, you will feel so much better.

For years after Harvey's death, when dull moments fell over a gay demonstration and the old slogans felt thin, someone could shout, 'Harvey Milk lives!' and it would not be hollow rhetoric; Harvey Milk did live, as a metaphor for the homosexual experience in America.

—Randy Shilts
JOURNALIST

On January 8, 1978, Harvey Milk and hundreds of his rejoicing followers took a victory march from his small Castro Camera Shop down Market Street to City Hall. Despite the cold, persistent drizzle and gray skies, they basked in the warmth of success. Although a smaller, more formal ceremony would be held inside, Milk had requested that an additional outdoor program include the overall public. As he joined the ranks of the San Francisco Board of Supervisors, Harvey Milk became the first openly gay man to hold public office in the United States, a fact acknowledged world-wide.

Milk's persistent strategizing, grassroots campaigning and inspired speech-making had paid off. His charisma and clever political savvy combined with a clearly stated commitment to issues of labor, environment, transportation, childcare and most of all, championing human rights made him a people's favorite. But he served on the Board for only eleven months. In the late morning of November 27, 1978, the Monday following Thanksgiving, eight shots resounded through City Hall. Milk and Mayor George Moscone had been murdered by ex-Supervisor Dan White. Despite the cold that evening, tens of thousands of shocked citizens silently converged at the intersection of Castro and Market Streets. Gay and straight people, united in grief, followed what had been the Milk victory route less than a year before. Proceeding down Market Street with candles in hand and gathering at City Hall, they lamented the loss of a popular hero. That Candlelight March remains an annual event in San Francisco.

On the day before what would have been Milk's forty-ninth birthday, a jury found Dan White guilty of voluntary manslaughter, a much lighter conviction than expected. Outrage swept the city as Milk again became a focal point for the men and women he represented all too briefly. In what became known as the White Night Riot, many gays and lesbians became overnight activists—attacking City Hall, burning police cars and chanting in the firelight, "Remember Harvey Milk."

Photographed by Dan Nicoletta

Betty Berzon and Teresa DeCrescenzo

PSYCHOTHERAPIST/AUTHOR AND CLINICAL SOCIAL WORKER, ACTIVISTS AND LIFE-PARTNERS

Lesbians and gays need a concept of permanent partnership for our relationships, a concept that sends the message that heterosexual marriage does: these two people are bound together in love and in life, functioning as a family unit, and invested in one another's future. — Betty Berzon

Betty and I have been together more than twenty-one years, and long ago we made our commitment to family unity. It extends to the hundreds of gay and lesbian kids we care for. The fate of our community depends on our caring for each other. — Terry DeCrescenzo

Betty and Terry are beautiful role models of family values representing personal bonding, and loving outreach to others.

—Malcolm Boyd
AUTHOR AND
EPISCOPAL PRIEST

On October 16, 1971, Betty Berzon looked up at the falling down wreck of a Victorian mansion smack in the middle of busy Wilshire Boulevard in Los Angeles. The sign on it proclaimed that it was the "Gay Community Services Center," the first of its kind in the world. Berzon had originally thought that she and the other madcap planners of the Center were naive to think that any government official or wealthy gay person would stick his or her neck out to become involved. However, Berzon and the other founders persisted, using guerrilla tactics to do the impossible. Today, the Center is the largest gay and lesbian service organization in the world. Berzon went on to found the Southern California Women For Understanding, to head up the National Gay Academic Union, to edit the ever-popular *Positively Gay,* and to write *Permanent Partners.* And Terry DeCrescenzo's deep and loving commitment to her partner has been a mainstay of Berzon's seemingly endless ability to continue her work in gay and lesbian activism.

In May 1989, Terry DeCrescenzo stood alone at the podium in front of the Los Angeles Community Redevelopment Agency desperately trying to get funding to save three Gay and Lesbian Adolescent Social Services (GLASS) homes from foreclosure. Eighteen gay and lesbian kids would be returned to the streets if she failed. Outraged citizens spoke one after another against funding: one prominent citizen remarked that he wanted to help teens, but "not these, they brought it on themselves." DeCrescenzo pleaded with the committee not to see this as a gay activist issue, but to respond instead to the lives of these children whom *no one* wanted. They listened quietly, then voted unanimously to approve funding. GLASS is America's only licensed facility for long-term residential services for gay and lesbian youth. Today, there are five GLASS houses, dozens of GLASS foster homes, and an extensive outreach program for the hundreds of gay and lesbian children still on the streets of Los Angeles.

Betty Berzon and Terry DeCrescenzo live with their three dogs in a house filled with mementos of their adventures in activism, where they entertain gay and lesbian people from all over the world.

Photographed by Suze Lanier
Courtesy Berzon/DeCrescenzo

105

Perry J. Watkins

FORMER U.S. ARMY SERGEANT
We won! We won!

Standing on the footsteps of the Ninth Circuit Court of Appeals on a crisp fall morning in 1988, Sgt. Perry J. Watkins tasted victory. The long years of legal battles had been worth it, for Watkins had done something that nobody had done before: defeated the US military ban against gays in the military.

Unlike other gay or lesbian servicemembers, Watkins began his military career by telling the Army that he is a homosexual. Drafted at the height of the Vietnam War in 1968, Watkins truthfully completed the induction questionnaire, clearly marking "yes" after the question of whether he had homosexual tendencies. Fully aware of his sexual orientation but in need of young able-bodied men to fight in an already unpopular war, the Army decided to take Watkins.

Honesty about homosexuality was extremely rare in those days, but "telling the truth" was something Watkins' mother had taught him from the very beginning. "I really didn't mind being in the Army," says Watkins. "What I didn't want was for them to kick me out for being gay, so the very first thing I'd tell my commanding officer was that I was gay and that I did female impersonations." As an openly gay soldier who had always dreamed of being an entertainer, Watkins found in the Army a sophisticated audience of friends and comrades who enjoyed his drag performances, many of them done on military bases, and often at the request of military officers.

From 1968 to 1983 Watkins reenlisted five times, serving two tours in Korea and almost eight years in Germany. In 1984, however, the Army finally got around to enforcing its policy, and discharged Watkins on the grounds that homosexuality was incompatible with good military service. With the help of the ACLU, Watkins decided to challenge the military regulations that prevent gay and lesbian Americans from serving their country. Although he was not the first to challenge the military regulations concerning homosexuality, Perry's case made significant in-roads in challenging the constitutionality of discrimination based on sexual orientation.

There are a lot of people who don't feel that they can really be who they are, and that was the remarkable thing about Perry. That he could just be who he was and then to have the courage to decide to fight for the right to be himself.

—Harold Robinson
GAY MOVEMENT
OF AFRICAN DESCENT

Rita Mae Brown

AUTHOR
If you can't raise consciousness, at least raise hell.

Rita Mae Brown came to New York City in the winter of 1965 with little more than the clothes on her back and a ferocious determination to rise out of the grinding poverty of her Southern upbringing. Her life, like the work with which she is most readily associated, would indeed turn out to be a classic American success story, but with an openly lesbian twist.

After losing her scholarship and being expelled from the University of Florida for civil rights activities and sexual adventuring (when confronted about her support for Blacks by a Tri-Delta sorority sister, Brown said that she didn't "care if I fall in love with a Black or a White or a man or a woman or an old or young person"), she went to New York to study classics, English, cinematography, and women. Along with her studies, she wrote poetry, helped form the Student Homophile League at NYU (where she was one of the few students to use her real name), contributed articles to various leftist and feminist publications, which were later collected in *A Plain Brown Rapper,* and co-founded the city's first women's center. An early member of NOW, she was eventually forced to resign because her views were too controversial. Frustrated by both gay male sexism and feminist heterosexism, she turned toward lesbian separatism. In the early 1970s, she helped to found the groups Redstockings and Radicalesbians, and for a time joined the separatist collective, known as the Furies. In between her political activities, she managed to earn a Ph.D. in political science, lecture at various colleges, and nurture the creative spark for which she is now best known.

Brown's open lesbianism and the all-embracing quality of such novels as *Six of One, Southern Discomfort, Sudden Death,* and *Bingo,* have established her appeal well beyond the lesbian and gay community. Brown put the personality in politics long before it was chic to do so. That alone may have guaranteed her lasting success. But her name is practically synonymous with *Rubyfruit Jungle,* the 1973 novel that may go down as the most famous lesbian coming of age story ever written. Yet she responds to her status as the lesbian laureate with typical audacity: "Next time anybody calls me a lesbian writer," she told *Publishers Weekly,* "I'm going to knock their teeth in. I'm a woman and I'm from the South and I'm alive, and that is that."

Brown's special talent for blending her feminist political views with her traditional notions of family earns her a unique niche in American literature.

—Carol M. Ward
BIOGRAPHER
AND CRITIC

Gerry Studds

U.S. CONGRESSMAN

Our struggle for equality is the last great chapter in the long history of civil rights in this country. That struggle will be won when each of us chooses to be open with those we know and love. It is ultimately our own self-respect—a force more powerful and more contagious than any virus—that will overcome the ignorance and bigotry that beset us. Together, we shall write that final chapter, and we shall all be free.

If you think your coming out was nerve-wracking, consider the coming out of Congressman Gerry Studds. In 1983, he stood before a hushed House of Representatives and revealed his sexual orientation to his colleagues, his constituents, and his country at the very worst moment of his life—just as the House was deciding to formally censure him for having had "improper sexual conduct" with a seventeen year-old male page. What for most people is a very private process became for Studds a terribly public trial by fire.

But that trial, which would have incinerated a lesser person, served simply to temper the veteran Congressman. He never apologized, saying, "I do not believe that a relationship which was mutual and voluntary constitutes 'improper sexual conduct.' " And he beat every odds-maker in Washington by handily winning reelection in 1984 with fifty-six percent of the vote. He has been reelected four times since, and not incidentally, has emerged as one of the most forceful and effective voices for lesbian and gay rights in the country.

Of course, it has been a long record of almost fanatical devotion to his constituents back home in coastal Massachusetts that has assured his seat in Congress (he even learned to speak Portuguese so he could better communicate with the mostly Portuguese-American fishing community of New Bedford). But Studds' careful attention to the concerns of his conservative district has never stopped him from championing the rights of lesbians and gay men. It was Studds, for example, who forced the release of secret Pentagon reports that came to the conclusion that the military gay ban was based on nothing but simple prejudice, and he has forcefully opposed the "Don't Ask, Don't Tell" compromise.

His seat on the powerful Health and Environment Subcommittee of the Energy and Commerce Committee gives him direct jurisdiction over AIDS policy, which he has used to oppose mandatory testing of health care workers, fight travel restrictions for the HIV-positive, and press for more AIDS funding. He is also a strong advocate for women's health issues: It was Studds who wrote the bill requiring that Pacific yew trees—which yield the breast cancer drug Taxol—be harvested rather than discarded. Yet for all his legislative successes, perhaps Studds' biggest achievement is his own political survival, proving that an openly gay politician can, with pride, triumph over almost any adversity.

Gerry Studds has been an outstanding leader on civil rights in the Congress for many years, and his leadership on causes of importance to gay men and lesbians has been indispensable.

—Edward M. Kennedy
U.S. SENATOR

Morris Kight

GAY AND LESBIAN RIGHTS PIONEER

All homosexuals have the potential for being gay. Some just haven't found out how to do it yet.

As a child in the small, Central Texas town where he was born in 1919, Morris Kight read through all thirty-two volumes in the library, and taught himself how to rebuild the engine of his father's old Model A. But Kight wasn't just curious about books and machines, he was also unusually aware of the larger issues in the life around him. When he opened a roadside diner at age sixteen to help earn a living for himself and his mother, he was arrested for "mixing the races" because he had served an African-American family who stopped in.

That was only the beginning. It is next to impossible to list even a small part of Kight's enormous achievements over seven decades of helping people and fighting for human rights. He counseled people with communicable diseases in the thirties, helped the NAACP integrate colleges in the forties, coordinated tuberculosis education in the fifties, led herbicide and napalm boycotts in the sixties, worked against the Vietnam War and anti-gay legislation in the seventies, and co-founded the Los Angeles Gay and Lesbian Community Services Center, coined now-common phrases like "non-gay," "physically challenged," and "people of color" in the eighties, and is now directing the McCadden Place Collection, of more than fifteen hundred posters and artworks of gay history.

Perhaps Kight's crowning moment was in 1978, leading and winning the fight against the Briggs Initiative, which if approved by the voters, would have resulted in the firing of any California teacher or school administrator who spoke of homosexuality as normal or healthy in any way. "If we blindly accepted our inferiority from people like John Briggs, Lou Sheldon, and Pat Robertson," he says now, "we would have been committing our own genocide. I breathed the most satisfying breath of relief in my life when we defeated the Briggs Initiative. It was one of the most important things I've ever done. They were saying that homosexuals were going to molest your children. It had devastating ramifications. When the voters rejected it, it was a major victory against such thought."

This soft-spoken man remains curmudgeonly stubborn, yet perpetually hopeful. "We have created the quickest nonviolent revolution in history," he says. "Twenty five years ago we were nothing. We may have a long way to go, but look at where we are."

Possessing the grandilo-quence of a Shakespearean actor, the fervor of a Bible Belt preacher, and the gentility of a Southern aristocrat, Morris Kight is to gay liberation what Bob Hope is to show business: peerless, tireless, fearless.

—Michael Kearns
ACTOR AND ACTIVIST

Photographed by JEB (Joan E. Biren)

Chrystos

POET AND AUTHOR

Whenever I start to judge another person, I stop and think, what is it about that person that frightens me? What is it that I am threatened by? Chances are it's really something in myself that I'm afraid of.

One day in January 1991, as Chrystos stood her ground in front of the federal building during a protest against the war in Iraq, she looked up and saw before her a policewoman on a horse. "She was doing her best to get that horse to stomp on me," says Chrystos. "And I realized I'd seen her before—in a lesbian bar. I asked myself, how can we make a community together, when we are on such different sides of this issue?" She often ponders this kind of contradiction. "See, on the other hand," she says, "I find it very disturbing in the lesbian community when people think that we all have to be the same. But what does that say about how I felt about that cop? Well, after I got through feeling angry with her, and judgmental, it occurred to me that, wait a minute— if that lesbian is willing to bust up protesters, maybe she voted for George Bush. That means he has to pay attention to her. That's interesting to me."

Chrystos likes to taste different viewpoints, imagining the thoughts and feelings of different kinds of people. It is taking the creative and the political, and mixing them up. "All writing is a political act," she says. "Even when I write lyric poetry, demanding to write what I want is political in and of itself." She sees metaphor everywhere in the gay and lesbian community, and in the world at large. "The homeless are a metaphor, I think, for despair just under the surface of American life. What does it say about us, when thousands of people are taking Prozac, when people need to take legal drugs just to go to work? I also think that AIDS is incredibly frightening, and that there is an unspoken fear pervading the gay and lesbian community. And fear is what keeps us from having access to compassion."

At age nine, Chrystos began writing "awful little rhyming prayers" to the Virgin Mary. She is from the Menominee, the Native American "People of the Rice," in the Great Lakes area, yet her father is an assimilationist, and Chrystos was raised in a Catholic home in San Francisco. Her education would take her through existentialism, to political activism, and to poetry. Her books include *Not Vanishing, Dream On,* and *In Her I Am.* In her newest work, *Interview,* she has created an older Native American lesbian. "The book claims a person who doesn't exist in lesbian fiction or Native fiction," she says. "She lives on the streets, drinking, with no money, and on the edge. I feel like I could be her if I had made different choices. I'm always conscious of that— that I have made choices in my life."

The honesty and fierceness in Chrystos' poems is, in her own words, a thunder that clears the air.

—Audre Lorde
POET

114

Richard Pillard

PSYCHIATRIST

What if sexual orientation is in fact a choice, and isn't genetic? Well, so what. Being gay is healthy and growth promoting, so gay people shouldn't be expected to join 'gay people's anonymous' or try to give up being gay. It would be much healthier to get a lover, and get on with being a happy, productive, and valuable member of society.

Richard Pillard is a true pioneer. At a time when most psychiatrists thought gay men and lesbians were sick, that they could change, and that they'd be better off if they did, he had the courage to say, 'This is wrong!' I regard him as a role model for all scientists interested in human sexuality.

—Dean Hamer, PhD

NATIONAL INSTITUTES OF HEALTH

In the early 1970s, Richard Pillard was the first psychiatrist in the United States to acknowledge publicly that he is gay. It was a truly courageous stand in a time when the American Psychiatric Association classified homosexuality as a mental disorder in their *Diagnostic and Statistical Manual (DSM)*. Pillard spoke out at symposia, and with other psychiatrists, lobbied the author of the *DSM*. In 1973, they succeeded in getting homosexuality removed from the *DSM* list of disorders.

Pillard has long believed that being gay is normal and natural. When he discovered that his brother and sister are also gay, his scientific curiosity was piqued. He began researching similar families, and his data on twins shows that lesbians and gay men have more lesbian and gay siblings than one would expect by chance. He believes this finding will help prove that homosexuality is a familial trait—a necessary condition in demonstrating a genetic link, which along with Dean Hamer's genetic research, and Simon LeVay's research into the hypothalamus, may eventually show that being lesbian or gay is biological. "After all, being gay is quite common," says Pillard. "There is probably even a selective advantage in having gay genes. A biological basis for homosexuality is ultimately irrelevant to the innate worth of gay people, or to the granting of civil rights. Yet it would make things easier because immutable characteristics are respected in the law." Some fear that discovering a genetic basis for sexual orientation may make it possible for parents to avoid having gay or lesbian babies. "Just because we have the scientific ability to produce only blonde, blue-eyed, and smart gods and goddesses," says Pillard, "doesn't mean that we should do it. That's a moral dilemma we will face well into the next century."

Pillard sees a rich history of gay and lesbian achievements, and has no doubt of the variety and value they add to society. "Chauvinistically, I like to think we're smarter," he says. "Lesbians are often natural leaders, for instance. Look at Dee Mosbacher, Roberta Achtenberg, or k.d. lang. All of them are noble dykes of great character. Music, literature, and art have all been enriched by gays and lesbians well beyond our numbers. It's as if God said, 'We need more art and music. I know—I'll create gay people!' "

Linda Morales

ACTIVIST

In 1986, I sat down with my mother and discussed my participation in a gay and lesbian class action suit against the State of Texas. She asked me why I wanted to tell the whole world about my lifestyle. I responded, 'Not the whole world, just Texas.'

Linda Morales thought that she would be denying her mother's moral teachings if she didn't participate in the lawsuit challenging the Texas homosexual sodomy law. Even so, her mother was uncomfortable with the public nature of her stand. But eventually, her mother told her, "I've always known you to have deep convictions and that it's important for you to stand up for them." Morales then joined four others in the suit, and agreed to be the named plaintiff in Morales, et. al vs. the State of Texas. "It was important for people to know that an Hispanic female was involved in our lawsuit," says Morales. " It didn't have to be Linda Morales, I just wanted someone who was a woman and an Hispanic."

Morales is not only a lesbian activist, she is also involved in Mexican-American and women's issues. "The lesbian and gay community is not immune to the ills of the larger society," she says. "And it was because of the racism and sexism in the gay and lesbian community that I put my name on the lawsuit." It was an important statement. Her case was eventually thrown out, but only because the court ruled that another case, England vs. the City of Dallas, had already established the legal basis for overturning the Texas sodomy law.

No matter. For Morales, the case was a victory—another step in a long road of using adversity to overcome discrimination. Even as a child, when her mother told her that girls shouldn't play the guitar, Morales taught herself. In Uvalde, her small southwest Texas hometown, where Mexican-Americans were expected to speak English, Morales was paddled in front of her fifth grade class for speaking Spanish. Yet in high school, she became the first Hispanic female elected student body president. And three months after she became involved in the Mexican-American Democrats de Houston, Morales was elected president despite the fact that this group is not a gay and lesbian organization.

Of her two brothers and one sister, only Morales' younger brother is heterosexual. "My kid brother has a lot of my father in him," she says. "He is very accepting and supportive. He's proud of me and I'm sure if my father were alive today, he'd be proud of me too."

Linda Morales is a rare, singular, unique person. If only I could bottle her energy.

—Yolanda Navarro
Flores
TEXAS HOUSE MEMBER

Elizabeth Birch

CORPORATE ATTORNEY
The heady possibility of freedom is in the air.

When the issue of extending benefits to domestic partners was raised at Apple Computers in 1993, the two worlds of Elizabeth Birch collided. As world-wide chief litigation counsel for Apple, her professional role would be to defend company policy. Yet as a lesbian living openly in a long-term committed relationship, and as a board member of the National Gay and Lesbian Task Force, Birch felt a responsibility to the gay and lesbian employee group Apple Lambda, and served as an unofficial advisor during the long process of drafting the group's proposal to extend benefits. Birch decided it was worth risking her job to fight for equality. "Though there had always been gays and lesbians in the company," she says, "they didn't feel valued as whole employees."

Birch decided to put it to a test after returning from the Clinton Inauguration with Apple CEO John Scully. "It was so inspirational. John came back filled with the spirit of democracy in action," says Birch, "and I came back realizing that after the dark years of Reagan and Bush, hope was still alive." Birch worked with Apple Lambda and the company's human resources department. She set up a meeting with Scully and privately informed him how easy it would be to implement the plan.

On the day of the meeting, the room was jammed with employees, all prepared to make impassioned pleas. But Scully upstaged them all by readily agreeing that formal recognition of domestic partnerships was an important step for Apple, a company long known for progressive policies, and that gay and lesbian employees are fully valued. "It was very emotional," says Birch. "There were a lot of tears. For me it was especially moving because having the coverage was not negotiable, and a key element to my continued commitment to the company. It was a transformational moment—another reminder of how important it is to take high risks at major moments."

Later that year, Scully marched with Birch at the March on Washington, leaving little doubt that pressing for civil rights is always a risk worth taking.

I consider Elizabeth to be a good friend. She's been instrumental in bringing a full understanding of gay and lesbian issues not only to Apple, but to many other corporations in this country.

—John Scully
FORMER APPLE CEO

Photographed by Paul Chinn

Written by Samuel Bernstein

Barney Frank

U.S. CONGRESSMAN

It finally got to the point where I knew it would be better for me if I came out. And I was right. It was wonderfully positive for me personally—and I have to tell you, the response from voters and my colleagues wasn't negative at all. In fact, almost everyone I've talked to says they had a better experience coming out than they thought they'd have. I am convinced most of us believe there is more homophobia in America than there really is.

When Republican Congressman Newt Gingrich spread a false rumor in June 1989 that Speaker of the House Thomas S. Foley was gay, Congressman Barney Frank, the first openly gay member of the United States Congress, was incensed. Frank knew that if he didn't threaten retaliation, the Republicans would continue unilateral shelling—so he dropped his own bomb, declaring that if they didn't back off from such dirty tricks and innuendoes, he would name closeted members of the Republican party. "I wasn't bluffing," Frank says, "but I don't know if I would have actually made good on the threat. Mostly I was just angry." The next day, after extensive media coverage, GOP Chairman Lee Atwater publicly apologized. Frank's hard-nosed move had paid off.

With a razor wit, a pragmatic grasp of political realities, and agile debating skills, Frank has evolved into one of the pre-eminent deal makers in the House. Though his negotiated compromise on the gay and lesbian military ban issue was unpopular with some in the gay community, Frank didn't think twice about it. "I knew I was right," he says. "The difficult thing about the military ban situation was realizing that we were going to lose if we didn't find a middle ground. That was hard. But I knew reaching a compromise was the best thing. A lot of people disagreed with me, but I'm used to disagreeing with people on my own side."

While proud of what the gay and lesbian community has accomplished, Frank believes there is still much work to do. "We have mistaken effective self-expression for political action," he says. "The March on Washington was great, and important as self-expression, but it didn't accomplish much politically. We need to write letters and lobby effectively. It doesn't matter when a million people march if only fifty thousand write to Congress."

Frank has lived with Herb Moses for five years. With Clinton in office, they receive invitations to the White House in both of their names, and Moses attended Tipper Gore's 1992 tea for Congressional spouses. Though at times uncomfortable with being held up as a role model—"What if I pick my nose or something?" he jokes—Frank thinks of his relationship with Moses as a very positive image. They do what other couples do in public: holding hands sometimes, and kissing. They know it makes a difference.

Congressman Frank has shown the world that gay and lesbian people can not only govern—but govern with excellence.

—David B. Mixner
POLITICAL CONSULTANT

Reno

PERFORMANCE ARTIST

I guess I always figure everybody knows I'm a lesbian. But the big deal for me in coming out is that I had to swallow years and years of hatred that I felt for my oppressors. The important thing is for me not to knee-jerk my reactions to them! So I'm the one who has to fight my own prejudices. Ain't that a kick in the ass?

At a recent media event, writer/performer/social critic/rabble-rouser Reno found herself unexpectedly advising Vice President Al Gore on stage technique while they were both waiting to go on. She marveled at how far mass consciousness had changed from her early days as an auto mechanic and member of a San Francisco feminist theatre collective. "Al Gore was backstage telling me a story 1 hadn't heard about feminists switching voice boxes on Barbie Dolls and G.I. Joes. 1 felt *bathed* in acceptance!"

As the uncompromising center of her solo performance pieces, *Rage and Rehab, Reno Once Removed* and *Reno Besides Myself,* Reno attacks anyone who tries to marginalize her. "We queers don't fit-in in the obvious ways," she says. "We make things harder for people who need their tunnel vision." Breaking stereotypes both within and outside of the gay and lesbian community is an essential part of her work, and it is a message she brings to rural parts of Ohio, Texas, Pennsylvania, and New England, where gay and lesbian people often feel isolated. Even in a community close to New York City, a gay man recently thanked her for "saying what nobody else has ever said around here."

A fixture of New York City's downtown performance scene, Reno roars her indignation at hypocrisy and injustice like a woman on the verge. Long on the cusp of major stardom, she has a tendency to resist success, to the point of self-sabotage, for fear of diluting her real essence: a volcanic life force blessed with a razor-edged wit, a stirring intelligence, and a compulsive honesty—which often comes at a great cost. "1 try to punch a hole until 1 can get to the truth," she says. "1 look for places where we can change things, where we can bite and have it mean something." Reno candidly exposes her vulnerability and encourages others to do so as well. She is a recovering alcoholic but sees her real awakening as a "coming out from killing myself," finding the power to turn away from the suicidal feelings that are common to many in the gay and lesbian community, particularly teenagers. But coming to terms with her own prejudices against the majority world, or as she calls them, "people with attaché cases," has allowed for greater understanding on both sides. Ask Al Gore.

Reno is so out there. I mean she really puts people on the edge. It's a caged animal thing. She's dangerous; there are times she scares the audience, not with threats, but by being completely uninhibited about her personal life.

—ROLLING STONE

Vito Russo

WRITER AND FILM CRITIC

You really can be political, outspoken, and who you are, and get away with it—if you're smart and talented. But if you're not smart and you're not talented, you can't get away with anything.

Standing in front of that still-new, magical mob known as a gay pride rally in June 1970, emcee Vito Russo had a problem. The crowd of mostly young gay libbers began yelling back at an older drag queen who had begun yelling at them. All sideburns and bell-bottoms, Russo grabbed the microphone and somehow managed to quell the volatile mix of hurt, outrage, and rowdiness before introducing the entertainer, a show-stopping newcomer by the name of Bette Midler. Russo's timing, as always, was impeccable.

In the wake of Stonewall, Russo played a key role in forming the Gay Activist Alliance. He shouted at gay-rights zaps and wrote incisive essays, reviews, and letters to the editor. More diplomatic than doctrinaire, Russo earned the trust of lesbians, straight women, militants, and closet cases. His stature zoomed in 1981 with publication of *The Celluloid Closet,* still the definitive text on homosexuality in the movies. Detailing the screen extremes of gay people as pathetic jokes, suicides, or monsters, he indicted Hollywood's unwholesome influence on generations of lesbians and gay men. He also indicted his own community, declaring in his introduction, "We have cooperated for a very long time in the maintenance of our own invisibility. And now the party is over."

Jobs ranging from bath house clerk to film preservationist at the Museum of Modern Art had carried him toward his eventual status as the Siskel-and-Ebert of the gay world. He reviewed films for *The Advocate* and wrote features—his prose always a hip balance of culture and relentless politics. "Hollywood has perceived over the years that it really is socially unacceptable to be racist or anti-semitic," he said in 1990, "but never in the history of movies have screenwriters felt more comfortable being anti-gay."

Over the years, Russo was one of the few politically minded journalists able to win the confidences of celebrities for the gay press. Lily Tomlin (for whom he also wrote comedy), Whoopi Goldberg, and the Divine Miss M are just a few of those who called him friend as well as interviewer. At the more than one hundred fifty universities and colleges where Russo lectured, he inspired a new generation to political wakefulness. After his AIDS-related death in 1990, his many friends couldn't quite let go. Rita Mae Brown called him "a marvelous gadfly on the gilded haunches of the Hollywood lion," and Lily Tomlin is working to fund a documentary film based on *The Celluloid Closet.* The world seems somehow less vivid, less of a celebration, without him.

Vito, dear, I'm gonna miss him. But in his name, among many others, I'll continue the fight against this fuckin' disease.

—Whoopi Goldberg

ACTRESS

126

Photographed with Lily Tomlin by Gene Bagnato

RuPaul

SINGER

In ten years I see myself in the White House. Before I go there I'm going to insist they paint it pink. Then it'll be the Love House. Talk about decorating that sucker! Miss Thing Goes to Washington!

RuPaul has single-handedly made it cool in American pop-culture to be a flamboyant, outrageous drag queen. Dominating MTV with the number-one single *Supermodel,* and generating more phone calls from a Black Entertainment Television appearance than anyone since Diana Ross (with most of the callers delighted), RuPaul is a big African-American empress, with big blond hair—Dolly Parton eat your heart out.

Deconstructing the lyrics of *Supermodel* doesn't take the efforts of a Susan Sontag. RuPaul sings about working that runway, checking out your *saviore-faire*—how when you walk into the room, everybody has an eye on you. The hit song is a paean to fabulousness that would make it easy to assume that the star has an ego to match the size of the wig. But that's not it at all. Dressed in a red, white, and blue Wonder Woman outfit to perform at the 1993 March on Washington, RuPaul stood backstage declaring, "I'm just like everybody else. I think the American public should realize that we are really all the same. We all want to be loved, respected, and feel like we belong somewhere. Is that asking too much? No! I love America too!"

With *Back to My Roots,* RuPaul explores not just African-American hair, but heritage, in a way that makes the singer's Supermodel status something closer to profound. The star also has definite ideas about drag, and believes everyone should try it at least once. "What you learn is how much emphasis we put on the outer layers, when what counts is on the inside. And girl..." RuPaul takes a long pause for effect, "Straight men will go after anything in high heels and a wig. Put them on your dog and you better lock up your old man. The force of drag is amazing! Talk about power dressing!"

This diva of dance music is quick to point out a main philosophy in life: "You want to know what RuPaul stands for? What I get behind and support? Do not write a check that your ass can't cash. Hello. Good bye. Click. Dial tone!"

What can I say about Ru? She's into giving, getting, and spreading luuuvv. Ru is six feet, seven inches, but with heels, hair and attitude, she's going through the roof.

—Traci Jordan
MTV NETWORK

Ron Nyswaner

SCREENWRITER AND PLAYWRIGHT

An artist's first responsibility is to tell the truth as he or she sees it. You really get into trouble if you try to please some imaginary committee.

Something of a media frenzy in the gay community greeted the opening of *Philadelphia*, the first major studio release to tackle AIDS and homophobia. The public, gay and straight, waited in long lines to see the movie and afterwards left moved, red-eyed, and quiet. It didn't matter. Many angry gay columnists and op-ed writers spoke of a bitter disappointment with the film, and came down hard on director Jonathan Demme and writer Ron Nyswaner. No less an august Movement figure as Larry Kramer, called *Philadelphia* a failure.

Maybe Nyswaner should have expected it—the gay press has a reputation for cannibalizing its own—but he was caught off guard by the controversy. He is an introspective, spiritual man who lives in upstate New York, and he strongly believes in a world where everyone has a place. "Larry Kramer is a great American. His anger has done a lot of good," says Nyswaner. "And there's room for ACT UP, room for chaining ourselves to buildings, but also room for reaching out neighbor to neighbor, and for being kind and tolerant." Nyswaner was particularly bewildered, even saddened, by the criticism leveled at the depiction of Tom Hanks' family as being too supportive of Hanks, and of his relationship with Antonio Banderas. "My boyfriend Alan Amtzis and I have been together for sixteen years," he says without a trace of defensiveness. "Our family is extremely loving and supportive. What's so unrealistic about that?"

Nyswaner sees his movies at his local mall cineplex, and he wrote *Philadelphia* for that audience— in hopes of bridging some of the differences separating gay and straight people. "I'm so touched by some of the letters I've gotten from people who never realized that hating gay people is a sin," he says. "We have to keep changing public perceptions of us. You know, Vito Russo said that he thought gay artists had to stop making gay art—that we should look beyond ourselves to see everyone's issues instead of just our own. I really think that's the truth."

Philadelphia went on to achieve enormous box-office success and Nyswaner was nominated for an Oscar. "Making the movie was an amazing experience," he says. "We met so many real-life heroes who are dealing with AIDS every day of their lives. I think we were all changed forever."

My life will always have two parts: before Philadelphia and after Philadelphia.

—Tom Hanks
ACTOR

Photographed by David Morgan
Courtesy Morgan

James Dale

EX-EAGLE SCOUT, BOY SCOUTS OF AMERICA

The problem with the Boy Scouts isn't that I am gay; it's the fact that I was proud to be out and happy with who I am. There are thousands of gay youth and young adults in the Boy Scouts of America, but most aren't openly gay and I was. For me, coming out wasn't just about telling a few close friends; it was about being myself all the time.

By age eighteen, James Dale had earned thirty merit badges from the Boy Scouts of America, he had attained the elite rank of Eagle Scout, become an assistant scout master, and was in constant demand as a speaker at Scout fundraisers. But in 1990, a local paper ran a picture of the New Jersey native speaking, as then co-president of Rutgers University's Lesbian and Gay Alliance, at a conference on gay and lesbian youth. Almost immediately afterward, Dale received a vaguely worded letter from the BSA informing him that he no longer met the organization's leadership standards and that his membership was terminated effective immediately. No explanation was given—and in violation of the Scouts' own rules, no hearing was held.

It was at that moment that the lessons the Scouts had taught Dale about honor and integrity came fully into focus. He put his BSA gear away, and engaging the Lambda Legal Defense and Education Fund, filed suit against the Scouts for discrimination. "The Boy Scouts taught me that you should stand up for what you believe in," he says, "and that's what I'm doing." The BSA have contended that Dale's homosexuality disqualifies him from being an effective role model. "I'm the same person I was then, if not better," he says. "But they think that because I'm publicly, openly, and proudly gay, that things are different. They're not."

Although there have been subsequent challenges to the BSA's unwritten policy on gays, Dale's case was only the second of its kind and is a highly visible test of New Jersey's civil rights law barring discrimination based on sexual orientation in housing, employment, and public accommodation. As its defenders are quick to point out, the BSA is a private organization, but the legal challenge rests on the fact that it uses public spaces. The case also comes at a time when the far right has become fiercely defensive about just such bastions of "traditional" American values as the Scouts caving in to the "homosexual agenda." But by standing firm against injustice, Dale is exercising a very traditional American right—testing the democratic accessibility of our institutions.

In his ongoing legal battle with the Scouts, and in his current championing of gay rights and AIDS issues, Dale remains confident of himself and of his convictions—becoming just the kind of hero the Boy Scouts of America would be proud to call their own.

James represents the best in lesbian and gay youth. He has contributed to the community around him and reflects the values of commitment and honesty, making other people's lives better—which he may well have learned in the Boy Scouts and through his family—but has redoubled as an openly gay young man.

—Evan Wolfson
LAMBDA LEGAL DEFENSE

Photographed by Jill Posener

Dorothy Allison

AUTHOR

I try to write really complicated and dangerous characters that leave you with a contradiction. I write to save my own life, and so that young people will have hope.

Dorothy Allison grew up in a world where she saw violence directed at women who loved other women. There was no name in those days for the women portrayed in her stepfather's pornographic magazines—women who were always ugly and violent. There was no name for her great aunt, who wore overalls and worked as an auto mechanic—a woman who was raped and murdered when Allison was very young. When she got "crawly, hot feelings" just looking at another woman, she felt like her only choice was to become someone who she was not, or to hide who she is. She assumed that she would have to become the Baptist equivalent of a nun, or change the world. After her first sexual liaison behind a Trailways bus station in Orlando, Florida, Allison assumed that the best she could hope for was to find a "reasonably tolerant woman" who was not abusive.

While that outlook was very bleak, Allison credits her survival, and her realization of greater possibilities, to the feminist movement. It was in the movement that she began to understand that all the oppression she had experienced as a woman and as a lesbian was not her fault: She was not the evil monster her background had led her to believe. At the same time, the political education she gained from the feminist movement exposed the painful reality of class oppression. Because of such class distinctions, claiming her identity as a lesbian feminist was never a simple task.

Yet the difficulty and complexity of her experience is what gives bloom to the work—Allison's books speak with the brave voice of a soul fighting toward freedom. She has written powerful fiction that challenges: Her first book, *Trash,* won two Lambda Literary Awards, and her second was the National Book Award-finalist and Ferro-Grumley Prize-winning *Bastard Out of Carolina,* which sometimes makes booksellers wince when they have to say the title aloud. But saying things aloud is sometimes what matters most.

There is much to admire in Dorothy Allison—her skill as a storyteller, her ability to use her pain and make it a source of strength is outstanding.

—THE VILLAGE VOICE

136

Written by Stanley E. Ely

Richard C. Failla

NEW YORK SUPREME COURT JUSTICE

I think it's important to be there wearing those black robes. There are people who don't think of themselves as homophobic, but unconsciously they say and do things that truly are. I, as a judge, am there to call them on that.

In 1970, just out of military service in Vietnam and beginning his legal career as a new assistant district attorney, Richard Failla discovered that another lawyer was extorting money from gay men entrapped by the police in New York City. When he confronted the colleague, she threatened to expose Failla's homosexuality. It was a crisis moment for the then thirty-year-old lawyer. In that era, a man risked being excluded from the New York state bar simply if known to be gay. "I saw my career shot," said Failla, remembering the incident years later. "But after some sleepless nights, I decided I just couldn't live in this kind of terror. I even realized how much a part of the oppression I was myself."

Choosing to stand up to that unscrupulous attorney's threats did not ruin Failla's future. He went on to become a senior trial attorney in the Manhattan District Attorney's office and in 1985 to receive an appointment as Judge of New York's Criminal Court. In 1989, capturing endorsements from the Democratic, Republican and Liberal parties, he was elected to a fourteen-year seat as Justice of the Supreme Court, State of New York. He was the first openly gay person to do so. Relishing the irony, Failla pointed out that Police Plaza, the site of his induction as judge, was in the very neighborhood once at the center of police entrapment of gay men.

Failla's partner of twenty years, Richard Gross, died from complications of AIDS in 1992. Failla also died of AIDS, in 1993 at age fifty-three. He is remembered as a youthful, elegant man who felt at ease as a role model to lawyers and young law school students; who worked to upgrade legal representation for indigents; and who lent his considerable energy to community groups, serving on the original board of the Gay Men's Health Crisis and on the New York State Health Department's AIDS Advisory Council.

Had he lived, Judge Failla would have served another decade on the New York State Supreme Court. He saw a bright future for gay people in the law and believed many more would serve on supreme courts and state appellate courts across America.

Judge Failla's election to the New York State Supreme Court is an event of historic significance. It is a testimony to the success of commitment and perseverance in the face of resistance, serving as a clarion call to the justice system that it can never afford to ignore a segment of a population it purports to serve.

—Mario Cuomo
NEW YORK GOVERNOR

137

Alison Bechdel

CARTOONIST

Cartoons can be remarkably subversive. They look so harmless, but they sneak up on you. I really love it when people will pick up one of my strips because it looks fun, and then suddenly they're in the middle of this lesbian universe. It's got to change the way they see things.

One hundred years from now, historians investigating American lesbian life at the turn of the twentieth century will undoubtedly find rich source material in Alison Bechdel's comic strip *Dykes to Watch Out For*. In fact, Bechdel sees her work as a kind of record of the times. "I think of my strip not only as the story of my characters' lives," says the thirty-three-year-old Bechdel, "but as a sort of archive, a chronicle of my generation, and a repository for the ephemera of our daily lives."

Since the cartoon first appeared in one-panel form, in the now-defunct New York-based *Womanews* in 1983, *Dykes to Watch Out For* has been providing timely, deft, and humorous commentary. Now a relatively lengthy twelve panels long, the strip appears bi-weekly in over forty-five gay and/or lesbian, feminist, and alternative publications in the United States, Canada and the United Kingdom. In addition, Bechdel's five books of her well-loved cartoon have sold over 75,000 copies world-wide and have won her two Lambda Literary Awards.

Bechdel's strip is an honest, accurate portrayal of lesbian life, according to its legion of fans who respond to the strip because the characters take on lives of their own. Her many readers follow the exploits of the ethnically and otherwise diverse *Dykes* gang, which includes Mo, hard-working women's bookstore staffer and tenacious whiner; Lois, her hard-playing pal committed to non-monogamy; Ginger, perennial grad student; and Sparrow, crystal-wearing therapy enthusiast. Bechdel's comic strip world also includes Clarice and Toni, the cartoon's professionals, complete with Volvo and artificially inseminated newborn baby boy. Since she first gave birth to this motley group, Bechdel has shown them dealing with life in a contemporary lesbian community with all its politics and dyke drama, its peak moments and quotidian details.

When not drawing the next *Dykes* installment, Bechdel occasionally tours with her slide show, covering topics ranging from the traditional sexist representation of female cartoon characters, to drawing as therapy. But the strip is her first love. "What I want," she says, "is to grow old with my characters. I want to stay current with what younger lesbians are doing, but what an amazing thing it is to be able to chronicle my own generation. It's a wonderful job."

Alison could be the one to really break things open for gay and lesbian cartoonists. Her strip is both political and hilarious, and she has invented such a great cast of characters. The issues she deals with are universal and open to everyone.

—Nicole
Hollander
CREATOR, SYLVIA

138

Jim Kepner

ARCHIVIST

Gays mostly believed that we have no part in history. We were left out of history. It's as if we weren't there. My position is yes, we do have a past, and it helps to know how we've been shaped in order to know where we can go from here.

In 1942 a twenty-year-old Texan named Jim Kepner arrived in San Francisco, "looking for a door to come out through from what only later became known as the closet." He wanted to be an activist in an era when the idea of lesbian and gay organizing was unheard of, when homosexuality was looked on as a dark, dirty secret.

"An overwhelming majority of gays believed we were sick," he recalls. "As large a majority—overlapping—believed we were sinners. " But Kepner didn't accept either belief. By the fifties, when he found his way into the first gay organizations then getting started in Southern California, he was exploring what became his passion: Collecting gay and lesbian literature, information and memorabilia. That small personal collection grew into the International Gay and Lesbian Archives in West Hollywood, one of the most extensive lesbian and gay collections in the world.

With over 20,000 books, tens of thousands of newspapers and magazines and files on more than 5,000 organizations (including material that exists nowhere else), the Archives charts a history that the young Kepner hardly dared believe could be possible. At a political protest during the forties, he asked a gay friend, "Do you think we could march like this someday?" "No," the friend replied. "Not in a thousand years."

The friend was wrong. And Jim Kepner has no doubt that history matters.

God bless Jim Kepner. I couldn't have finished my book without him. His monumental archives of lesbian and gay books, organizational records and personal effects has aided countless researchers. For that alone he deserves a chestful of medals. He is our Claudius. He has seen everything, at least in the West, and jotted all of it down. His legacy is crucial: Extroverts fade, scriveners endure.

—Stuart Timmons
AUTHOR

Charles Busch

ACTOR AND PLAYWRIGHT

My artistic aesthetic was fully developed at the age of seven. I watched Norma Shearer in Marie Antoinette, and I was just her! I forced my aunt to run around town trying to find a movie theater still showing I Could Go On Singing so I could be with Judy. But it took me fifteen years to realize that what was unique about me as a child could become a career.

Vampire Lesbians of Sodom. Just the title alone was enough—funny, thrilling and campy, with a hint (all right, more than a hint) of wickedness. It was the forty-minute skit that started Charles Busch and his Theatre-in-Limbo on a wild ride in 1984. Audience response at the Limbo Lounge in Manhattan's East Village was so ecstatic that Busch began writing a new play for his repertory company every three weeks, starring as the leading lady. Some fans would attend every performance, chanting the lines along with the actors and giving each entrance a spectacular ovation. *Vampires* would move to a bigger house and go on to become the longest running non-musical in off-Broadway history—and *Psycho Beach Party, The Lady in Question* and *Red Scare on Sunset* would confirm Busch's success.

But getting there wasn't easy. Never mind the fact that *any* career in the entertainment industry is a Sisyphean struggle; Charles Busch is a gay man who has earned his greatest fame playing women. Squint just a little and he *is* Joan Crawford—face greasy to suggest a wrong-side-of-the-tracks, dead-end life—striding through a turgid Warner Bros. drama, crying out, "I'm going to get myself *out!* Get what *I* want! And *no one's gonna stop me!*" Busch certainly has that kind of determination and drive. Yet there is also about him a quiet grace and an unusual mix of fantasy and pragmatism. Scratch the surface and you find an artist.

While in college, Busch worried that his childhood dreams of a theatre career might not pan out. His newly discovered sexuality was everything to him, yet the more he explored his gay self, the less he was able to imagine playing male roles. It was extremely painful for he had to make a choice. Many men might have hidden, masked their uncertainty with a butch facade—*I can be Biff! I'll be the best, straightest damned Biff you ever saw!* But Busch knew that his path lay within his imagination, where he was creating fantastical, extremely complex movie parodies—both losing and finding himself in a fictional world.

He would go on to start a theatre company, tour with a one-man show and do every kind of temp job imaginable. He would work himself to the bone and realize his dream of making a living in the theatre. Behind it all is the clear voice he began listening to long ago—a voice that told him to be himself at any cost, to find his own art. It is the voice inside that can make vampires sing.

That the lady in question is a man soon becomes beside the point. What matters here is that the performer in question is a star.

—Frank Rich
NEW YORK TIMES

143

Greg Louganis

OLYMPIC DIVING CHAMPION AND ACTOR

As a diver I was known for my strength and grace. One day, I'd like to be known as a person who made a difference beyond the world of diving.

Growing up, Greg Louganis was called "retard" and "nigger" because of his dyslexia and dark complexion. He was also called a "sissy." Often harassed after school, he spent much of his childhood alone, seeking refuge in the rocky hills of his El Cajon, California, neighborhood. Diving saved him. "It was something that I could take pride in—and I was good at it," he says. "It was the one way I could respond to the people who called me names. I was terrible at fighting back with words or fists, but I could show them all by diving."

Louganis' artistry and skill earned him a silver medal in 10-meter platform diving at the 1976 Olympics in Montreal when he was only sixteen. In the years that followed, he won scores of national and international titles and awards, including a total of four Olympic gold medals in the 1984 and 1988 Olympics for both platform and springboard diving.

And if anyone ever had questions about Louganis' spirit, there was no doubt after the world watched him gash his head on the diving board during the preliminary round in three-meter springboard diving at the 1988 Olympics, only to see him return minutes later with stitches in his scalp to complete two more dives and qualify for the next day's final competition. Again, he took the gold medal. Resilience, perseverance, and breathtaking skill, combined with humility, warmth, and sense of humor, have earned Louganis the admiration of people around the world.

For those who recognized Louganis as a gay person, his accomplishments had special meaning. Many young people wrote to Louganis expressing their appreciation. He also heard from those who were frustrated that he didn't step forward and speak publicly about his sexual orientation. "I was always out to my family and friends," he says, "but I was never comfortable discussing that part of my life with the press or the general public. Keeping the secret was often painful. "It was always the toughest for me when parents would bring their kids to meet me and say, "I want my child to grow up to be just like you." I always wondered if they'd still feel that way if they knew I was gay."

Louganis recently completed a six-month run in the Off-Broadway show "Jeffrey," and is currently working on his autobiography, which will be published by Random House in early 1995. "I'm planning to talk openly about my life in the book," he says. "But it has taken me a long time to reach the point where I have the confidence."

Photographed
by Annie Leibovitz
Courtesy Leibovitz

145

Written by Karen Ocamb ◊ Photographed by R. Scott Hitt, M.D.

Diane Abbitt and Roberta Bennett

ATTORNEYS

It was a very, very special thing to go into the White House as a guest. Not only because it's unbelievably beautiful and filled with a sense of history, but because the last time we were there, we got arrested protesting the President's compromise on gays in the military. It speaks to what this country is all about, that the Administration can then go and value the contributions we've made by inviting us to dinner.

"Want to dance?" Roberta Bennett asked Diane Abbitt, her longtime life and legal partner. Abbitt looked around. "Let's wait," she replied. If they were going to become the first openly lesbian couple to dance together in the White House, Abbitt wanted to make sure it was a slow dance.

Bennett and Abbitt waltzed around the East Room ballroom that night, January 5, 1994, as representatives of Access Now for Gay and Lesbian Equality (ANGLE). They had been invited by President Clinton to a small "thank you" dinner for prominent campaign supporters. The story is quintessential Abbitt and Bennett: "It seemed like the most natural thing in the world to dance with the woman I love," says Abbitt. "But another part of me was interested in making a statement."

The couple has been making statements—and history—for over twenty years. As lesbian mothers in the political dark ages, they endured harsh discrimination and vowed to change that for future generations. During the reign of Florida orange juice shill Anita Bryant, they quickly realized that the courts and "checkbook activism" were key to creating legislative protection and public acceptance. They started one of the first law firms targeting the lesbian and gay community, testified on behalf of the California bill that decriminalized homosexuality, created a lesbian task force for the Los Angeles chapter of NOW, and helped form the Municipal Elections Committee of Los Angeles to raise funds for gay-friendly politicians. They have helped make gay men and lesbians into a credible political force.

"But so many of our friends were ill," says Bennett. And they were devastated by their friend Peter Scott's AIDS-related death in 1989. "It took a tremendous amount out of us, emotionally and physically," says Bennett. Grief-stricken, they took a year off from activism. But with the 1990 elections approaching, and noticing that "gay rights were getting short shrift because of AIDS," they leapt back in. They co-founded the Gay and Lesbian Victory Fund and ANGLE, raising over $3 million for Clinton, which helped to solidify the first gay voting bloc, which in turn translated into a half billion dollars in new AIDS funding—and a small but vital symbol: at the epicenter of American power, dancing cheek to cheek.

Diane and Roberta are community leaders. They contribute their time, energy, love, and resources and they have made a difference. They have also been friends, supporters and advisors to me as I have embarked on my campaign for governor.

—Kathleen Brown
CALIFORNIA STATE
TREASURER

146

Andrew Sullivan

EDITOR AND WRITER

When I write an article on the federal budget, I'm doing something for gay equality because everyone knows that an openly gay man is doing it. I look forward to the day when our sexuality will cease to be an issue. I want us to join society as equals.

In December 1990, subscribers to *The New Republic,* the influential Washington journal, were startled to see the magazine's cover printed in black with a pink triangle in the center. Above the triangle in bold white letters were the words, "Gay Life, Gay Death." With his controversial cover story on AIDS that questioned the gay article of faith that AIDS has unified the gay community, deputy editor Andrew Sullivan served notice to his magazine's audience of politicians and opinion-makers that gay issues covered from a gay perspective were now a part of mainstream journalism.

Sullivan is now editor of *The New Republic,* and, barely into his thirties, is considered the whiz-kid of political journalism. Coming from a modest background in England, Sullivan was the first in his family to attend a university. It wasn't until he came to the United States with a fellowship to Harvard that he felt free of British society's "covert signals" to pursue a stereotypical "gay career." "I love the United States," says Sullivan. "Sometimes immigrants see better than natives what a great tradition we have here of individual liberty."

Being openly gay is not a big deal for Sullivan, and he feels that this is true for most gay people of his generation. "I've always been out in my personal life," he says. "My circle of outness just became bigger as my position became more public." He acknowledges being an anomaly in the power circles of Washington, where few gay or lesbian people are vigorously forthright about their sexuality. But when a *Time* reporter concluded an interview with him by asking, "Oh, and by the way, you're gay, right?" it didn't occur to Sullivan to turn the question aside. "My experiences as a volunteer with Whitman-Walker, a local AIDS clinic, made it harder for me to play games with the closet," he says. "It reminded me of what matters, and that to live honestly is the only option."

Sullivan has published a number of other articles on gay issues in *The New Republic* and is now planning a follow-up to "Gay Life, Gay Death." His conservative views on such hot-button issues as outing and the effectiveness of AIDS activism have not always met with a welcome reception in the gay community, but he is sanguine about prospects for reconciliation with other opinion makers in the community. "People have mellowed about the diversity of views," he says. "We weren't used to internal debates, but are more used to it now. Dialogue is a good thing. These issues are too important to be reduced to an official line."

A new editor who defies the old conventions, Sullivan has brought a cutting-edge quality to the magazine's reporting on homosexuality.

—TIME

149

Written by Bruce Mirken

Lyn Duff

YOUTH ACTIVIST

I lay on the concrete floor, dazed, my head throbbing where it had hit the wall. Drying the tears from my eyes, I pulled myself into a sitting position. Then I saw it. Scratched in the paint on the Seclusion Room floor was a triangle, a small, pink triangle. We are everywhere, even in this place.

At the age of fifteen, Lyn Duff lived through an unimaginable nightmare. Her mother committed her to a locked psychiatric institution where she was forced to undergo "therapy," including hypnosis, isolation, physical restraints and powerful drugs—all intended to "cure" her lesbianism. "They drug you out, make you really tired and cloud your thinking," she recalls. "They'd say, 'When you think about girls sexually, push that thought back into a closet in your mind, then lock the door and throw away the key.' " The word-association exercises she was taught equated all sex, both homosexual and heterosexual, with "the pits of hell."

Six months into her confinement, Duff found her chance to escape when she got a weekend pass to visit her mother in California. On her first night home, she fled, making her way to San Francisco. For several months Duff was on the streets, in and out of youth shelters, and hiding with friends. But with the help of two agencies, the National Center for Lesbian Rights (NCLR) and Legal Services for Children, she was able to get a court order giving guardianship to a lesbian couple, Rena Frantz and Ora Prochovnick, whom she had met through the NCLR. Duff started a new life with her two lesbian moms, their infant daughter, a gay male roommate, and assorted pets.

At seventeen she now devotes much of her time to "fighting the laws—so that no kid, gay or straight, ever gets locked up again." With the help of three friends who like many gay teens underwent experiences similar to hers, she has started *24-7: Notes From the Inside,* a publication for teens who are, or have been, in mental hospitals. The title refers to twenty-four hours per day, seven days per week clinical supervision. Some copies also go to the youths' parents. "We hope it will open their eyes," she says, "to what's really going on."

Lyn has a way of reducing what seems to be a major trauma down to the simplest terms. It was amazing, the insight she gave me. I can't wait to see what she turns out like as a young woman. I can't wait.

—Sass Nielsen
GLADD/LA

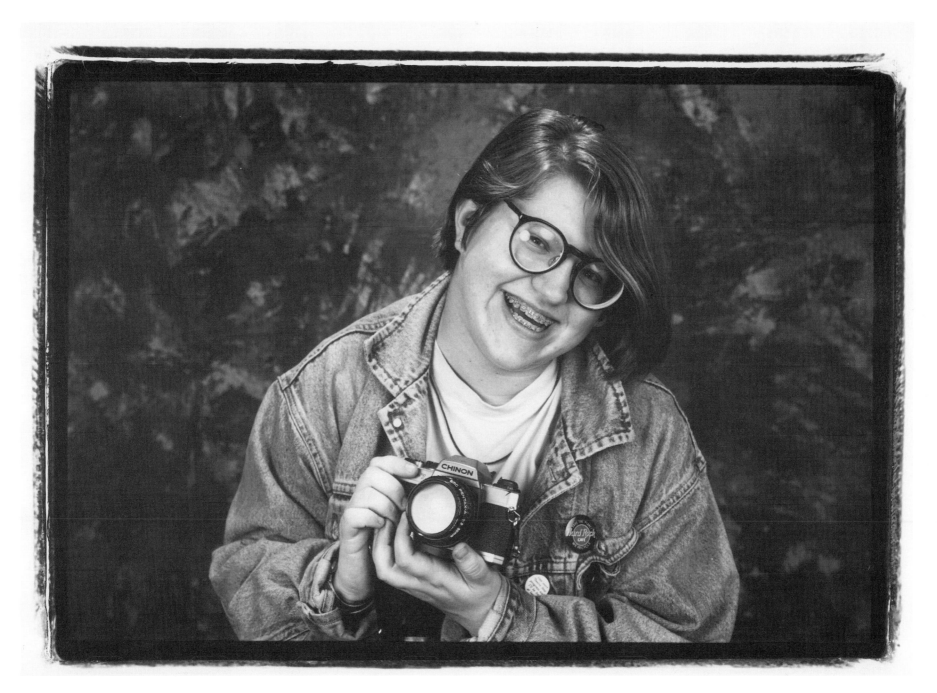

Photographed by Nick Lammers
Courtesy Anderson/Maupin

Terry Anderson and Armistead Maupin

ACTIVIST AND WRITER

I get so tired of these stories about, 'Oh, the torture and torment of coming out.' There's no torment in coming out. The torment is in being in. —Armistead Maupin

Armistead is fifteen years older than me, but we came out at roughly the same time, which we always say makes us the same 'gay age.' I think that's one reason why we're so compatible. —Terry Anderson

In 1985, when Terry Anderson met his lover-to-be, he was a twenty-six-year-old student at Georgia State; he'd been out of the closet since age seventeen, when he left home for a life he could live on his own terms. One day, as president of his school's gay alliance, he went to the airport to pick up a visiting writer named Armistead Maupin. Anderson had never heard of Maupin's *Tales of the City,* but when he laid eyes on its renowned author—he faked it. "We had plenty to talk about," says Anderson. "I felt I'd known him all my life."

Maupin had come at least as far as Anderson: Scion of an unrepentant Confederate family, he served a stint in Vietnam, and worked in a North Carolina radio station as something of a protégé to Jessie Helms. By the time he had become the satiric yet loving chronicler of San Francisco—and in 1992 the author of *Maybe the Moon,* a novel about a tough, sexy thirty-one-inch-high Hollywood actress—Maupin had started calling coming out "the final act of manliness." He encouraged friends like Rock Hudson and Ian McKellen to abandon the closet, and he allowed *Tales* to be filmed only with assurances that the main homosexual character wouldn't just be the "witty gay neighbor down the hall."

Anderson is now Maupin's business manager, amanuensis, and quite literally, his inspiration. When Maupin's fictional hero, Michael Tolliver, tested positive for HIV in *Significant Others,* the author drew heavily on his lover's firsthand experience with the virus. And Michael's "mixed marriage" with the antibody negative Thack Sweeney is similarly autobiographical, though, as Maupin puts it, "Thack's sassiness is much more Terry's than mine."

Armistead Maupin and Terry Anderson live in the epicenter of AIDS, where the massive earthquake of the plague has swallowed more lives than the San Andreas faultline ever has. Being out as gay men has shaped their lives, and so has the harder honesty of being a couple forthrightly confronting HIV. They live with one implicit, brave, and earthmoving motto: No secrets. If some couples take each other for granted because they can't imagine being separated by death, these two know they could share a final chapter someday. So they hold on to the precious, the sweet, and live their life together like a well-written, very open book.

Broad shoulders, hearty laughter, and the joy that comes from believing Christmas is every day because you can be how you are: This is Armistead Maupin and Terry Anderson.

—Anthony Godby Johnson
AUTHOR

Sherry Thomas

PUBLISHER

In 1965, I was embarrassed, lonely, and afraid when I went to the Washington, D. C. public library looking for anything that would tell me something about myself. I made an amazing discovery when I found Mary McCarthy's book, The Group. *It was about women at Vassar College, some of whom were like me! I wasn't alone anymore. I even had a name—lesbian. For the first time in my life I knew everything was going to be okay.*

Sherry Thomas is creating the nation's first permanent public facility and collection for gay and lesbian culture. Her meteoric rise to executive director of the Library Foundation reflects not only her skill and foresight, but also her dedication and concern for this remarkable project and its potential for human enlightenment.

—James C. Hormel
PHILANTHROPIST

As a young child, Sherry Thomas wanted to be a United States Senator—a simple dream. But when the Vietnam War broke out she became an anti-war activist instead. She climbed into a Volkswagon bus and moved to California, eventually becoming a farmer in Mendocino. From this rural outpost, she started *Country Women*, an early lesbian and feminist magazine. In 1978, she opened the Old Wives' Tales book store in San Francisco. By the early 1980s, it was one of the largest women's bookstores in the United States. In 1982, she took over Spinsters' Press, a lesbian book publisher, and published fifty titles over the next ten years. Thomas joined the Library Foundation of San Francisco in 1990 and eventually became executive director. The Library Foundation has raised over two million dollars to endow the Gay and Lesbian Center that will be part of San Francisco's new library. This project had the total support of San Francisco's movers and shakers. "It blew my mind," Thomas says, "to have the richest people in town stand at a cocktail party and say, 'We're doing the most wonderful thing. We're putting a gay and lesbian center in our new library. And now we're using it as a model to get other ethnic communities involved in the library.' It's a shining moment for the library."

The Gay and Lesbian Center will house the largest publicly held collection of gay and lesbian material in the world. It will include every book containing a gay or lesbian character published in English since the early 1800s, complete runs of all gay and lesbian periodicals going back to the 1920s, gay and lesbian films, and an extensive gay and lesbian archive.

"We will have state-of-the-art electronic access to our collection," says Thomas. "Our patrons will be able to take a reproduction quality photograph of a single frame from a movie home with them. We are going to reproduce our rare books and manuscripts so that the reproductions can circulate. And we will be on-line throughout the world!"

154

Photographed by Anne Dowie

Paul Rudnick

WRITER

I had no idea how audiences would respond to Jeffrey, whether they'd be willing to accept repartee and big-time Gershwin amour amid the nightmare of AIDS. But I knew that any portrait of Manhattan life in the nineties would have to be a blend of the highest farce and the most devastating tragedy, laced with the gay style that has allowed a ravaged community to survive with its wisecracks and wardrobes intact.

Paul Rudnick had written close to fifty drafts of the play that became the acclaimed comedy *Jeffrey.* He had seen countless readings. "I wanted to write a play that dealt with AIDS that didn't end up in a hospital room," he says. Jeffrey, the play's title character, has given up sex in response both to ten years of the AIDS crisis and to the frustrations of romance in general. "As others have pointed out, the renunciation of love and physical contact has served such playwrights as Aristophanes, in *Lysistrata,* and Shakespeare, in *Love's Labour's Lost,*" he says. "But while these are both fine works, their authors did not benefit from the satiric fodder of red ribbons, hoe-downs for AIDS, and memorials hosted by Siegfried and Roy." Then early in the play, Jeffrey meets Steve, his perfect match. "I had originally thought that if Steve were HIV-positive, the play wouldn't be funny," says Rudnick. "But that became the interesting challenge. The moment someone tests positive, his life *isn't* over: he can *still* fall in love; he can *still* make wisecracks."

So, after all the drafts, Rudnick went back to square one and decided that Steve would be HIV-positive. It was important to make Steve a vibrant and sexy character, who was never a victim. Still, how would the community respond? It was enough of a gamble to use humor in writing about AIDS without being accused of trivializing a holocaust. Rudnick was nervous and exhausted on New Year's Eve 1992, the night of the play's first preview. "When Tom Hewitt, the dreamboat playing Steve, announced that he was HIV-positive, the theatre fell silent," says Rudnick. "The audience was convinced that the play was no longer a comedy—yet seconds later they were howling again."

After a sold-out run at the WPA, *Jeffrey* moved to the larger Minetta Lane Theater and ran for more than a year, winning a 1993 Obie Award. Olympic diver Greg Louganis made his New York stage debut as a replacement in the role of Darius, the chorus boy from *Cats.* Successful productions were also mounted in Los Angeles and San Francisco. Rudnick, a consummate shopper and the author of the novel *I'll Take It,* as well as the play *I Hate Hamlet,* went on to write the screenplay to the highly subversive *Addams Family Values.* His current project *The Naked Truth,* is a satiric play dealing with a controversial visual artist.

I've known Paul all his life and he has always been my role model—but I don't see a lot of vacuuming.

—Libby Gelman-Waxner
PREMIERE MAGAZINE

Merle Woo

EDUCATOR

This is what it's going to take: the creation of a multi-racial/multi-sexuality feminist coalition for radical economic change: revolutionary integration.

Chinese-Korean American, socialist-feminist, and survivor of cancer, Merle Woo was thrust into mainstream activism when she was terminated from the Asian-American Studies Department at the University of California, Berkeley in 1982. Woo's dismissal was supported by one faculty member who asserted, "It is inappropriate for a lesbian to represent Asian-American Studies." Woo soon found herself in the media spotlight when she filed suit, charging four separate areas of discrimination: race, sex, sexuality, and political ideology. Her radical outspokenness outraged university officials, especially when she exposed their violation of UCB's own affirmative action policies. Although the university employed a plethora of defense attorneys, Woo won an out-of-court settlement, and was reinstated in 1984.

UCB again fired Woo in 1986, this time from the Graduate School of Education. Once again she prevailed, this time through union arbitration. In 1991 Woo received back pay plus an additional cash settlement. Woo viewed her fight against the university as representing the obstacles that every victim of discrimination must face, and her triumphs were monumental both for herself, and for the gay and lesbian community at large.

Woo is the author of *Yellow Woman Speaks: Selected Poems,* and has also been anthologized in several publications including *Tilting the Tower: Lesbian & Gay Studies,* and the classic text of empowerment *This Bridge Called Me Back: Writings by Radical Women of Color.* Currently, she teaches in the Women's Studies Department at San Francisco State University and is well recognized as a leader in Radical Women and the Freedom Socialist Party. Her tenacity and resiliency has been influenced by three philosophies which contribute to her vision: Clara Fraser's "revolution is intense compassion", Roque Dalton's "revolution will be an aspirin the size of the sun," and Assata Shakur's "revolution is about change, and the first place that change begins is within yourself."

Merle Woo proclaimed her lesbianism when most of us were only whispering the words, and when other Asian-American women did not dare even to name it in their hearts. She writes, she teaches, above all she fights, and she has quickened our lives with her courage, her wisdom, her endurance, and incredible revolutionary love.

—Sally Miller
Gearheart
WRITER

159

Written by Geoffrey Staples

Glen Maxey

TEXAS STATE REPRESENTATIVE

When I was first elected to the Texas Legislature, the big joke on the House floor was, 'You better move your seat or you're going to have to sit next to the queer.' In some ways, I'm glad that happened on my very first day. Most often, we can't shine a bright light on homophobia and discrimination because it's done behind our backs. But I got to walk into the legislature knowing exactly who told the faggot jokes, who was embarrassed by this blatantly bigoted display, and who wanted to help.

It was a bruising campaign. Even Anne Richards had advised him against it. His opponents tried to make an issue of his private life. The race received national media attention. But none of that mattered when in 1991, Glen Maxey became the first openly gay man ever elected to the Texas State Legislature. In fact, he was the first openly gay man to even *run* for a seat.

Maxey represents Travis County, which includes Austin, the state capital. His friend, Governor Richards had been worried that even if he were elected, he would have to be perfect on everyone's pet issue, or that he might be viewed as a single issue legislator—the "gay one." That didn't faze Maxey. "My objective," he says, "was to be the environmentalist, or the consumer advocate, who just *happens* to be gay." During his first term, he made legislative ethics reform his issue. When a colleague asked how he had the courage to take on the House leadership, he responded, "Once you've gone through the terror and the agony of coming out to your family, friends, and co-workers, standing in front of this legislature and introducing a bill is a piece of cake."

As he has gained political experience, Maxey has found new and even deeper connections with his gay constituents. "I've had teenagers walk up to me and say, 'When I grow up I want to be just like you.' When that happens, I get the message deep in my being," he says. "Or a sixteen-year-old gay young man who told me that because of my example he had decided to go into AIDS law. See, it's all about the fact that lesbian and gay youth desperately need role models so that they can envision themselves growing up to be what they want to be."

As long as I've known him, Glen Maxey has been an activist for the people. As a member of the legislature, he has been a fighter on a whole host of issues. I am proud that we have fought the fight together on the same side all these years. And I'm proud that he is my friend.

—Ann Richards
TEXAS GOVERNOR

161

Written by Samuel Bernstein

Malcolm Boyd and Mark Thompson

WRITERS, LOVERS AND LIFE-PARTNERS

There's something about the beauty and power of gay love. We build bridges between our differences, and honor the mystery of what we have. —Mark Thompson

When I'm introduced at functions with Mark, if someone asks me what I do, I like to borrow from the story about Tennessee Williams and Frank Merlo. I tell them, 'I sleep with Mr. Thompson.' —Malcolm Boyd

This is going to get mushy. No matter how one tries to put Malcolm Boyd and Mark Thompson on some sort of pedestal because of their extraordinary achievements (and make no mistake, they *are* extraordinary), it doesn't feel right to set the two of them in bronze with a distancing list of achievements. It is their love—a soulful, spiritual sense of belonging—with each other, and with the world, that defines them. They are romantic and intimate, intellectual and passionate. But that doesn't quite tell the whole story either, for they are also funny. Even silly. Ask the people at the restaurant in conservative Pasadena where they had their first date. During dinner Boyd casually asked Thompson to dance. He *casually* accepted. As they *casually* slow-danced between tables, they began noticing silverware clattering, chairs scraping, and people staring. It was then that the two men remembered that the restaurant had no dance floor.

After a two-year courtship, Boyd proposed on bended-knee and gave Thompson an Indian ring. For ten years they have shared not only their lives, but their work, and a commitment to riding the delicate balance of illuminating the universal through exploring the particular—which in terms of their writing means focusing on the special gifts they find in all gay people. To some, the couple is a study in contrasts: Boyd is an Episcopal priest while Thompson embraces a mix of Buddhist, Pagan and Radical Faerie philosophies; Boyd was raised on the east coast, Thompson on the west; Boyd is HIV-negative and Thompson is HIV-positive; and there is a thirty-year span in their ages. But to focus on their differences means missing the point—which in some ways, is the whole point.

The books they have written could fill a small library. Boyd's include *Are You Running With Me Jesus?* and *Take Off the Masks.* Thompson has been an editor with *The Advocate* newsmagazine for twenty years, and has authored *Gay Spirit: Myth and Meaning,* and *Gay Soul.* He also edited *Long Road To Freedom: The Advocate History of the Gay and Lesbian Movement.* As book people, human rights advocates, and gay men, Boyd and Thompson have spent much of their lives looking for deeper meaning, and searching for fresh air. In their journey they have found truth and they have found each other—and still, as the years pass, they dance.

Really, they are both priests. Mark is a shaman, a visionary, while Malcolm is an Episcopal one. The wisdom of blending the two visions together is clear to anyone with eyes.

—Paul Monette
AUTHOR

162

Jared Nall

ACTIVIST

A legless veteran in a wheelchair was waving a Bible and shouting, 'You'll burn in hell.' The protesters' children looked scared. One protester said, 'I love you,' like he could forgive my sins. We started chanting, 'Some of your kids are gay!' I saw the television cameras and got goose bumps.

When Operation Rescue in Dallas planned a large demonstration in opposition to President Clinton's attempt to lift the ban on gay men and lesbians in the military, Jared Nall knew he had to be there to counter the homophobia that would be on display. He had no idea, however, that he would be on the evening news or that every classmate of his would soon know he is gay.

Nall was a high school senior in Garland, Texas, who served as a mascot for his school team, the Patriots—at football games he wore a minuteman uniform, replete with musket and replica of the original Betsy Ross flag. After word spread of his public outing on television, many students either ignored him, or taunted him with the epithet "fudge-packer," and for the rest of the school year he ate his lunch alone. "Even my manager at work would tease me by singing 'And have a *gay* old time' from the *Flintstones,*" Nall says. "But each day I got through made me stronger and more determined to be out. If you're not out, you're hurting the cause." Later, as a college freshman he applied for a position at a restaurant and wrote "GLYA" and "ESLA" on his employment application as "outside interests." When the interviewer asked, Nall told him the letters stood for "Gay and Lesbian Young Adults" and "Eastfield College Lambda Student Association." All the interviewer said was, "Cool," and offered him the job. It was exactly the kind of response Nall had hoped to get by being honest.

Before the demonstration that changed his life forever, Nall had already been out to his family. "When I had first envisioned telling them," he says, "I couldn't imagine looking them in the face. But I had to do it—I had to tell them that I'm okay, that it's society that has the problem." Though his mother had a difficult time initially with her son being gay, she did what her mother had taught her to do in times of confusion: she prayed, then read, and learned all she could. "I feel guilty that I didn't take time to find out about gay people before this," says Joan Nall. "Other kids deserved better from me, and it took Jared to wake me up. He's one of the best people I've ever known, so how could he be anything but great?"

It's not easy for a young man to be out. Jared has helped his parents and other gay youths. His enthusiasm is contagious. I was thrilled to have him and his mom lead our group in the 1993 March on Washington, carrying the P-FLAG banner. Their smiling faces said it all— the power of family pride.

—Pat Stone

DALLAS P-FLAG
CHAPTER

Ivy Bottini

ACTIVIST

At the end of the Women's March on the Mayor's Mansion in 1969, I found myself boosted up onto an open stakebed truck with a microphone in my hand. So I started speaking about what had brought all these women out on an icy day in January and I found myself becoming one with the crowd, all of us together, standing behind the issues of the Women's Movement. And I guess I've been trying to define the issues and unify the crowds ever since.

Sparks flew in 1969 when Ivy Bottini, a founding member of the first local chapter of the National Organization for Women (NOW), presented a panel on *Is Lesbianism a Feminist Issue?* The wide press coverage that followed set off the first of the now-infamous "lesbian purges" in the ranks of NOW leaders. It was rumored by some that Betty Freidan personally engineered a whispered campaign of false innuendo that led to Bottini being voted from office in 1970—this despite the fact that Bottini had served as president of the New York chapter in 1968 and 1969 and had created Feminist Consciousness Raising, which boosted membership and was widely emulated around the country. "Betty never understood," says Bottini, "and still doesn't understand to this day— that until the Feminist Movement can shrug off being labeled lesbian, it will always be stalled by fear."

When Anita Bryant began pitching homophobia in the mid-1970s, Bottini experienced *deja vu:* Bryant was preaching the same discrimination, based on irrational fear, that had driven the purges in NOW. Bottini realized the full scope of the discrimination lesbians and gay men can be subjected to throughout society and determined never to be limited by others' judgments again.

Bottini has lived fearlessly ever since, and is always willing to speak out publicly as a lesbian activist, whether from stakebed trucks, hotel podiums, pressroom microphone banks, or the steps of city halls, state capitols or the nation's Capitol. She tirelessly works for gay and lesbian concerns, opposing homophobic ballot propositions that have plagued California since 1978, chairing statewide political campaigns, speaking as the four-term president of the Los Angeles Stonewall Democratic Club, representing the lesbian and gay community on the Governor's Commission on Aging, educating the American Red Cross on the value of donated lesbian blood; and on and on. The list of important causes she actively supports is virtually inexhaustible, with her clear message ringing through every act, both political and personal: "Come out! Live out! The closet is killing us!"

Ivy is a courageous activist with uncommon energy. In my political encounters with her, I always found that she stood out as a leader; on a human level she is remarkably engaging.

—Jerry Brown
CALIFORNIA GOVERNOR

166

167

Michael Denneny

SENIOR EDITOR, ST. MARTIN'S PRESS

Gay publishing seemed as if it might give me an opportunity to do something with a political dimension—beyond just making money or having a career. For me, a non-political life seems almost unhygienic. Improper.

More than once Michael Denneny's friends warned that he would ruin a promising future in publishing if he became known as a gay editor. Yet each time, Denneny ignored their advice. In the mid-1970s, when there was little gay publishing and still less corporate acceptance of a gay lifestyle, he joined the group inaugurating *Christopher Street* magazine. Convinced that a substantial market for gay books existed, he set himself a difficult job search: An editor's post with a publisher that would back his plan to develop a series of lesbian and gay titles.

St. Martin's Press agreed to Denneny's idea and still supports his vision seventeen years later. As senior editor at St. Martin's and general editor of its Stonewall Inn Editions, he has edited at least one hundred thirty gay and lesbian titles, including such familiar names as Paul Monette, Randy Shilts, Larry Kramer and Edmund White. Over the past two decades Denneny has been instrumental in the "coming out" of gay publishing, from a time when there were "so few gay books that every gay man read each one," to 1992, when a total of twelve hundred lesbian and gay titles were published; from a time of no gay book stores to over fifty today.

As a young boy in his parents' poor, noisy Rhode Island household, Denneny joined eight book clubs and created his own world through reading. During anti-war demonstrations at the University of Chicago, he was befriended by famed academics Hannah Arendt and Harold Rosenberg, in whom he found "examples of intellectuals who knew how to relate thinking to reality."

Those politically explosive years of the late 1960s led Denneny to the ongoing dual track of publishing gay books and fostering acceptance of a gay culture. He is a founder of both the Publishing Triangle, a professional organization of lesbians and gay men in publishing, and the National Lesbian and Gay Book Month, occurring every June.

Denneny has seen gay literature blossom, yet he has also witnessed the havoc AIDS has wrought on much of the gay culture he has worked for decades to nurture. "I've lost many friends, men whom I've watched grow up," he says. "I've taken work to edit and sat at the bedside of some who were comatose. If I'm there, I'm sure the person knows he's not alone. It's good for them—and good for me."

My career is due almost solely to the assistance of one person: Michael Denneny. Neither of my earlier books would have been published except for him; this third book reflects his ongoing confidence and support.

—Randy Shilts
CONDUCT UNBECOMING

Photographed by Alain McLaughlin/Impact Visuals

Urvashi Vaid

ATTORNEY AND POLITICAL ANALYST

I don't fight to live in the lesbian community. I fight to live in the whole world.

Brilliant activist. Fiery orator. Insatiable listener—most of the time. In March 1990, Urvashi Vaid, executive director of the National Gay and Lesbian Task Force, refused to listen when President Bush rose to speak before a polite luncheon crowd of the National Leadership Coalition on AIDS. Minutes into his speech, Vaid stood and held up a sign: *Talk is Cheap—AIDS Funding is Not*. The back of the sign read: *Remember Gay People with AIDS*. Stunned silence was followed by instant commotion, as the Secret Service led Vaid away. She joined the ACT UP protesters outside.

"I was appalled at that Administration's negligence on AIDS," says Vaid. "And I was infuriated that Bush was giving his first major speech on AIDS to a large gay and AIDS group, and yet everyone felt constrained to act. Virtually everybody there was an executive director of a national organization—about sixty of whom had been arrested during a World AIDS Day demonstration three months before. I felt I couldn't let the opportunity slip by. This was the gay mainstream saying it was fed up."

As personally rewarding as this "defining moment" was, Vaid is proudest of having co-created the NGLTF Creating Change Conference in 1988, which allows grassroots gay and lesbian activists from around the country to "talk politics, build skills, and inspire each other." At the time, Vaid was only thirty years-old, the movement's youngest national leader. "When we first started Creating Change, we had two hundred people. In our 1993 conference in Durham, North Carolina, we had twelve hundred, and the hot topic was the North American Free Trade Agreement," says Vaid, now a political analyst, and at work on a book about the future of the lesbian and gay movement. "That's the challenge. We have to fight to get out of the gay ghetto. I don't mean to put it down. It's my shelter, my home. I work to build it, and it sustains me. But we should claim any issue that involves our lives. Ultimately, all issues are connected."

Urvashi has reached a broad spectrum of people with her knowledge, skill, and wisdom. She knows how to raise money, and how to raise hell.

—Alan Hergott
ENTERTAINMENT
ATTORNEY

James C. Hormel

PHILANTHROPIST

I'm living proof that the world goes on even after you come out of the closet. I've lived in both the gay and non-gay worlds. I have ten grandchildren. My role is to find opportunities to bring people from both worlds together. I couldn't do that from the closet.

James C. Hormel makes things happen. The American Civil Liberties Union had been struggling for three years to develop a gay and lesbian project, but had only raised half the money needed. They were at an impasse. Hormel provided a challenging grant, and the balance of the money was raised in a matter of weeks. This was only the beginning of Hormel's long commitment to supporting gay and lesbian causes. In 1981 he worked with his close friend Sam Puckett to organize the Gaycare event to promote volunteerism. The Volunteer Bureau of San Francisco signed up more people that night than they typically get in one year. Later, Puckett, ill with AIDS, wrote the first book on AIDS in the workplace. "Sam made enormous contributions without getting any attention or credit," says Hormel. "So, we worked with KQED-FM to create *A Night of Volunteering* honoring him. The program featured interviews with Sam and the executive directors of numerous non-profit organizations. Due to its success, KQED ran it annually for five years."

The list of Hormel's activist and philanthropic achievements is endless: He was a founding board member of the Human Rights Campaign Fund in 1981, host for the 1984 Democratic National Convention in San Francisco, a Clinton convention delegate and platform committee member at the 1992 Democratic National Convention, and was one of the first openly gay people to serve on the San Francisco Chamber of Commerce board in 1993. And he doesn't keep quiet, no matter where he is. At a White House dinner, he was seated with Joint Chiefs of Staff Chairman General Shalikashvili and Hormel took the opportunity to ask him about gays in the military. The general responded that it wasn't matter of "whether," but only a matter of "when."

Hormel is currently working to create the Gay and Lesbian Center in San Francisco's new library, which will be the largest publicly held collection of gay and lesbian material in the world, and is challenging the San Francisco register to support his AIDS service project, Stand Up To Be Counted. "In the late sixties and early seventies, the few references to lesbians and gay men in the press were couched in terms at best clinical, and at worst derogatory," he says. "When an ex-Marine foiled an assassination attempt on Gerald Ford, he was a hero for a few days until it was discovered he was a gay man. Now, we are in the news daily. We must seize this opportunity to define ourselves."

It is a blessing to cross paths with Jim Hormel. He epitomizes the respect, dignity, gentleness, and strength which distinguish great leaders. Jim has successfully brought the force of his personality to bear on AIDS, the arts, and human rights, and he has done so with a special grace and goodness which makes him a truly uncommon hero.

—Nancy Pelosi
U.S. CONGRESSWOMAN

Phranc

FOLKSINGER

Coming out wasn't a choice that I had. The choice I had was to survive or not to survive. As soon as I found out, I came out. I came out to myself and to the world—to my family and everybody all at the same time—for me that was a survival tool. I think I probably would have died if I hadn't come out. I really do.

Sporting a crewcut and armed only with an acoustic guitar, Phranc marched into the lion's den of the Los Angeles punk scene and sang about everything from fascism to Martina Navratilova. Proudly calling herself a "Jewish lesbian folksinger," she was out in a scene dominated by mostly angry, mostly male kids. It didn't matter. She developed a wide audience of appreciative fans and recorded a number of albums. Now Phranc is everywhere—clubs, coffee houses, the Comedy Channel—full of spirit, energy, and grace.

By the time she was ten, Phranc had performed Hebrew songs for her family and had been influenced by the mixture of styles in her parents' record collection, mostly show tunes and Allan Sherman parodies. She first heard lesbian folksingers in her teens, came out at seventeen, and consulted Jill Johnston's *Lesbian Nation* as her style guide. "Then I went to San Francisco to find that new lesbian community," she says. "What I found was punk rock. It was a major turning point." Here was a creative community with a do-it-yourself ethic; like the older lesbians she had met, the punk rockers allowed her to be herself, but were also her contemporaries. Phranc played and sang with the now-legendary *Nervous Gender* and *Catholic Discipline*, but after the bands broke up she went solo. Songs like *Take Off Your Swastikas* typify her approach: in direct, honest, and brave language she confronts the fascist symbology of some punk rockers. Using the folk medium—ideal for her kind of storytelling—but infusing it with punk's intensity, Phranc forged her distinctive style.

Phranc kicked off the 1990s with *Hot August Phranc,* a show that combined her regular performance with a "drag king" set of Neil Diamond songs performed with tongue-in-cheek gusto. "I think humor is really important, but I do feel this responsibility when I'm Phranc with my guitar on-stage that I don't have when I am this other persona and it's very fun to just goof off on-stage and have a blast."

An unchanging theme in Phranc's work and in her public statements is the importance of being out and proud. "One of the reasons I've always been out in my work is I believe that young people who come to see me perform deserve to know that they can grow up and be whoever they are. It doesn't matter if they grow up to be straight or gay or lesbian. They can see somebody else who is out and who is living—successful and surviving—and having a *great* time."

After her concert, I realized I hadn't felt this giddily queer since cutting class to see Paul Morrissey-Andy Warhol films in high school.

—Robert Atkins
VILLAGE VOICE

Photographed with Holly Hughes by JEB (Joan E. Biren)

175

John Scagliotti

TELEVISION PRODUCER

We need to turn on the television and have a moment of us all being together. If there is national gay and lesbian television, we can have these 'national moments.'

It was John Scagliotti's belief in the importance of gay and lesbian history that drove him to create *In the Life,* the program about gay and lesbian life, now in its second season on PBS. It is the culmination of over ten years of determined effort by Scagliotti to make gay and lesbian television a reality. When the first episode aired in 1993, he thought back thirteen years to when he and producer George Page submitted a proposal for *Different Drummers* to the development department at WNET-TV, New York's PBS affiliate. Scagliotti had been building on his experience covering gay and lesbian issues as news director for WBCN Radio in Boston. But after expressing some initial enthusiasm, PBS became skittish about the possibility of losing government funding. After all, it was the beginning of the Reagan era.

But this time around, Scagliotti had confidence in community support. "After AIDS activism started happening," he says, "I sort of dusted off *Different Drummers.* I felt the community itself would put pressure on public television stations to air the program. We're more organized now. We have gay people who are demanding to get on local boards of PBS affiliates." And it worked—with no funding from PBS (everything comes from private sponsors and individual memberships).

In a nation where all too often lesbians and gay men don't know what's going on with their own community in other parts of the country, *In the Life,* has established a vital link. "I think it's very important to have that sense of community in a national way, and in some ways international," says Scagliotti. "That way we're not isolated anymore."

John is an explorer who took on uncharted territory. Quietly. Humbly. Swiftly. And our community is stronger because of his vision.

—Garrett Glaser
TELEVISION REPORTER

Photographed by David Morgan
Courtesy Morgan

Torie Osborn

FEMINIST AND WRITER

I had this sense that we had earned this moment—step by step, death by death, fight by fight. There was a definite sense that our time had come.

Striding into the White House on an April morning in 1993, Torie Osborn headed a contingent of activists for the first-ever formal meeting between the President of the United States and a group of lesbian and gay leaders. She had pushed hard to make the meeting happen. As the executive director of the National Gay and Lesbian Task Force, she had lobbied Apple Computer CEO John Scully, friend and boss of NGLTF Board Co-Chair Elizabeth Birch, who had then called his friend President Bill Clinton.

"And the walls came down," says Osborn. "Never had I been so driven about something in all my life. And never had I been as clear that something was historic. It felt to me like this was bound to happen." She believes the ninety minute meeting was important and meaningful, although it was at times contentious. "It was clearer to Clinton than to us that the gays in the military issue was headed for a debacle," she says. "Nonetheless, there was an intense degree of emotion and righteousness in the room—we are a people who deserved that meeting."

The road Osborn has followed is symbolic of that taken by many progressive activists from the 1970s to the 1990s. She was a women's music producer; worked on David Mixner's anti-nuclear Pro-Peace campaign; brought new power and services to the Los Angeles Gay and Lesbian Community Services Center as executive director, while bringing the huge organization up to gender and racial parity; and was on the front lines of five days of demonstrations after California Governor Pete Wilson vetoed AB-101, a gay rights measure. Osborn has also been a fiery and articulate media spokesperson against anti-gay violence and as an advocate for lesbian and gay youth. After her tenure at NGLTF, she stepped down to work on her own as a writer, thinker, and freelance activist.

John Scully speaks very highly of you.

—President Bill Clinton

SAID UPON MEETING TORIE OSBORN AT THE WHITE HOUSE

As powerful as the meeting with the President was, Osborn feels that speaking before nearly one million gays and lesbians at the March on Washington was the most personally "awe-inspiring" moment of her twenty-five years of activism. "I felt so lucky to be part of that occasion," she says, "which was filled with such exuberance and transcendent pride."

178

Tony Kushner

PLAYWRIGHT

I was ready to write a play about being gay which was set in contemporary America. The political soul of this country is now up for grabs and I wanted a work that would explore the position of the gay community within the context of this national struggle.

Angels in America: A Gay Fantasia on National Themes is Tony Kushner's apocalyptic view of humankind; a two-play, seven-hour masterpiece. The first part, *Millennium Approaches,* won Kushner the Pulitzer Prize for Drama, Broadway's Tony Award for Best Play and the London Evening Standard Award for Best Play. The second part, *Perestroika,* opened on Broadway in the 1993-94 season. Playing in repertory to sold out audiences, the two shows are a huge hit, and Robert Altman is set to direct the screen adaptation next year. *Angels* is an epic that covers miles of terrain: gay Mormons, AIDS, Roy Cohn, angels who are frustrated by a God who is on vacation, the practical realities of political evil, reasons to keep on living, and such problematic questions as why Jewish kids are named "Eric."

A complex and introspective man, Kushner is the son of musician parents who gave him political convictions and set him on a quest for truth. "I was surprised to find myself writing Roy Cohn as a sympathetic person," he says. "My family is liberal, Jewish, musical, politically aware—and Cohn was a central evil figure in American history. But I felt he was not a hypocrite—his seemingly unbelievable contradictions came from deeper implications."

Kushner is known for his breadth of theatrical vision, with an oeuvre covering freely adapted versions of the seventeenth century playwright Pierre Corneille's *The Illusion* and the early twentieth-century playwright S. Anasky's Yiddish drama, *The Dybbuk,* as well as *A Bright Room Called Day, Heavenly Theatre,* and *Slavs!,* a new play inspired by earlier drafts of *Perestroika.* He is highly political, and intellectual to boot, which might frighten off less-involved theatre audiences, but infuses his work with timeless importance. Oskar Eustis, co-director of the California productions of *Angels* has said, "Personally, 1 think that Tony isn't just the model for the next generation of American playwrights. 1 think he will be—and in some ways already is—the model for a generation of Americans." Kushner has easily and gracefully earned the mantle "Great American Playwright."

Daring and dazzling! Tony Kushner's Angels in America is the most ambitious American play of our time, an epic that ranges from Earth to heaven; switches between realism and fantasy, from the tragedy of AIDS to the camp comedy of drag queens, to the death, or at least the absconding, of God.

—Jack Kroll

NEWSWEEK

Virginia Uribe

PROJECT 10 FOUNDER AND DIRECTOR

Many boards of education are filled with spineless, cowardly, gutless individuals who at the slightest criticism fall apart at the seams. If they could just get it into their heads that public education serves all children, then they would want to protect all children.

In 1984, a seventeen-year-old Black openly gay student transferred to Fairfax High School in Los Angeles. From his first day he was physically abused by his peers, and verbally abused by both staff and students. With no support from school officials, he soon dropped out—another depressing statistic in the cycle of unrealized potential and lack of self-esteem endemic among lesbian and gay youth. He never returned to school, but through the grapevine earth science teacher Virginia Uribe heard of the situation. She began meeting with a group of twenty-five lesbian and gay students during their lunch period to talk about what had happened to the boy, and about their own problems and concerns. "Soon I realized the problem was bigger than me," she says, and gathering her courage, told her principal about the group. To her surprise, the principal told her, "We're public educators. We need to serve all of our kids. Go forward."

That was the start of Project 10 (named for the oft-cited statistic that ten percent of the population is homosexual), an on-campus program aimed at keeping lesbian and gay students in school, off-drugs and sexually responsible. Project 10 improves the self-esteem of lesbian and gay youth by providing accurate information and non-judgmental counseling. It also benefits the school's non-gay population by teaching students and staff to live peacefully in a diverse society.

"The most positive thing Project 10 has done is open up this area for discussion," she says. "We have to get it into schools, even if the school districts don't want to face it." Her program, developed ten years ago as an impromptu discussion group, has become a model for similar projects throughout the country. That's quite a tribute to this tireless woman who began teaching at Fairfax in 1959, but was herself closeted as a lesbian until 1984. Yet she sees it as only a beginning. "The challenge ahead is to broaden our visibility," she says, and she has plans to create a foundation which will serve as a nationwide research center on lesbian and gay youth.

Being associated with Project 10 has given me the same affirmation and future opportunities that all students receive. From feelings of hopelessness when I came to Fairfax, I now feel good about myself and look forward to a happy and successful future.

—Gregory Thomas Cartwright

VALEDICTORY SPEECH

182

Photograph Courtesy Uribe

Juan R. Palomo

JOURNALIST

I'm not feeling too proud of myself today. Paul Broussard was beaten to death with nail-covered two-by-fours in another hate-filled attack on gay people. Broussard's mother said she didn't understand how this could have happened to her son. Well, I can understand. I have listened in silence as a co-worker suggested going out 'to beat up some queers.' I have remained silent as an admirer urged me not to write anymore about fags, because my readers would be upset. I know that such things are a result of the silence of people like me. I feel a special responsibility to speak out because I have this forum and, because like Broussard, I am gay. I have to deal with the fact that unless people like me are willing to risk the comfort and safety of our closeted lives, we will never stop the hatred. I didn't know Paul Broussard, but I know I have a responsibility to ensure that Houston does not forget him, or how he died—or why.

When Juan Palomo wrote those words for the *Houston Post,* his column was censored by his editors. They didn't want him to come out in print, so they forced him to remove the part about his being gay. It was controversial enough that Palomo was so angry about the fag-bashing death of the young gay banker Paul Broussard. When word got out that Palomo couldn't *be* out, the *Houston Press,* an alternative paper, interviewed the columnist and wrote a story subtitled, "*The Houston Post's* Juan Palomo had something important to tell his readers. His own paper wouldn't let him, so we will." After the article appeared, Palomo was fired for disloyalty.

His firing made national news. The paper attempted to counter the embarrassing publicity by trotting out various establishment Hispanic leaders to show how inclusive and broadminded they are. That only triggered a flood of ethnic outrage. Palomo is the son of migrant farm workers from Mexico, and he continued working farms with his family until his last year of college. He may have been queer, but to the Hispanic community, by God he was *their* queer. Various Hispanic groups, along with Queer Nation, picketed the *Post.* Palomo's coworkers signed petitions and some even joined the picket lines.

Juan Palomo was re-hired. And his column in the *Houston Post* now deals with being gay—as well as with being Hispanic, being American, and living in urban Texas. His power comes from writing about what it means to be human.

Juan Palomo has become a symbol of the difficulties gay and lesbian journalists have to overcome once their sexual orientation is known. His attempt to come out publicly in his column was unprecedented and courageous.

—Leroy Aaron
NATIONAL LESBIAN
AND GAY JOURNALISTS
ASSOCIATION

185

Amanda Bearse

ACTRESS/DIRECTOR
I've lived a pretty blessed life.

Scores of cameras clicked and whirled on National Coming Out Day 1993 when Fox Broadcasting Company star Amanda Bearse strode into the conference room at the Los Angeles Gay and Lesbian Community Services Center to announce to the world that she is a lesbian. As she joked with the national press, the hardest decision she had in coming out of the closet, was deciding what to wear. "I stood there looking at my clothes," she says, "and said to myself, 'Amanda, you just have to come *out* of this closet!'" She chose a jacket, jeans, and her favorite T-shirt, inscribed *Hate Is Not A Family Value.*

Bearse plays the straight, ever-horny bank teller Marcy D'Arcy, comic foil to Al and Peg Bundy on *Married...With Children,* the breakthrough hit that launched Fox Broadcasting with a crude, trashy bang eight seasons ago. "When Marcy first encountered the Bundy family and saw how different and coarse they were, she thought she might be a positive influence on them," says Bearse. "But instead they've dragged her right down to their level." Bearse, who has been acting since high school—including a two-year stint on the ABC soap *All My Children* and the lead role in the feature film *Fright Night*—says *Married...With Children* is intended as a spoof. "It's almost anything for a laugh," she says. "And everybody on the show, every character, is subject to ridicule—mine included." In addition to acting in the series, Bearse has directed a number of episodes.

In March 1993 Bearse and her lover Amy Shomer, a television commercial producer, exchanged vows in a religious commitment ceremony at Pasadena's All Saints Episcopal Church. The couple is happily raising their adopted daughter Zoë.

Bearse is currently the only openly lesbian or gay series-regular on television—a distinction she hopes will become passé. Perhaps the fact that not one of her producers or any of the Fox executives has had a bad word to say about her decision to come out will change the perception of how impossible it is to be an openly gay or lesbian actor in Hollywood. Whatever happens, though, Bearse is not about to return to the closet. "I'm not in this business for personal validation. It's what I do and I'm good at it. But I'm a lot more than my job," she says. "And besides, when you have someone like Amy and a little baby girl, who needs anything more?"

Amanda Bearse is a rare Hollywood commodity. She was willing to lose her career rather than hide who she is. She since has become a dedicated activist and her career is flourishing. Amanda is an inspiration for all of us.

—Lorri L. Jean
LOS ANGELES GAY AND LESBIAN COMMUNITY SERVICES CENTER

Mel White

THEOLOGIAN

Jerry Falwell and I had just flown into San Jose, California. We were driving in our limousine to a church when we were cut off by a huge demonstration of gay people. They were angry because Jerry had said that AIDS was God's punishment on gays. As we went through the crowd, Jerry said, 'Thank God for these gay demonstrators. If I didn't have them to draw a crowd, I'd have to hire 'em. They give me all the attention I need.' I wanted to be outside demonstrating and there I was sitting inside that car. That was my point of shame.

Mel White has told my story and that of thousands of evangelical gay Christians: the terrified youth, the prayers for deliverance, the belated introduction to the concept of social justice, the inauthentic marriage, the suicidal depressions, the same-sex affair, the divorce, and at long last, the authentic relationship.

—Virginia Ramey Mollenkott

WRITER

Dr. Mel White told his wife he is gay the year they were married. With her support, he underwent exorcisms, ex-gay reparative therapy, and electric shock. Nothing worked. Eventually, he found himself hanging out around the corner from the West Hollywood Metropolitan Community Church, trying to get the courage to go in. By the time he finally went into MCC for the first time, White had developed an illustrious career as a ghost writer for such luminaries of the religious right as Billy Graham, Pat Robertson, Jerry Falwell, and Jim and Tammy Faye Bakker. He began leading more and more of a double life, and while still writing for Falwell, joined the Act Up demonstration at St. Patrick's Cathedral.

Then he did the unthinkable and came out to his former colleagues, including Falwell, Robertson, and Oliver North. Now none of them will speak to him. White had hopes for Billy Graham, but Graham has remained silent. "He didn't attack gay people, even when he sermonized on Sodom and Gomorrah," says White. "But he did a big rally in Portland, Oregon before the vote on anti-gay Proposition 9. I tried to get him to speak out against it, but he didn't say anything. He says he's not a political figure. I told him that justice is a spiritual issue and his silence was aiding injustice."

White doesn't mind getting arrested every once in awhile during demonstrations, and doesn't miss his old high-powered career at all. "Even if I were just ghost-writing autobiographies," he says, "I'd be part of the team that supports the enemy. As long as we stay closeted in homophobic churches, playing the organ, leading the choir, and giving our money, that's what we're doing: supporting the enemy. And keeping hate alive." White is now dean of the Cathedral of Hope Metropolitan Community Church in Dallas, Texas, America's largest gay and lesbian congregation. He monitors the religious right and is creating an outreach for gay and lesbian people. And his message is hitting the mark. After CNN broadcast the Cathedral of Hope's 1993 Christmas Eve Service, requests for help and information flooded in from throughout the world.

Jewel and Rue Thais-Williams

BUSINESS OWNERS, AIDS ACTIVISTS

Coming home to being whoever you are; accepting yourself, loving yourself, and being proud of your heritage, your gayness, and your community; and being proud of being an American—this is what we think is important in life.

When the Simi Valley jury returned a 'not guilty' verdict in the trial of the four white Los Angeles police officers charged with beating Rodney King, Jewel and Rue Thais-Williams both held their breath. They knew there would be trouble and they were right. Within hours, cries of "No Justice, No Peace" rumbled across the country. In Los Angeles a riot erupted, petrifying the city for days.

Her security service refused to come, so Jewel Thais-Williams stood guard alone to protect Catch One Disco, the Black gay club she opened in 1972. Over the years the nightclub had evolved into a community center and "safe space" for lesbian and gay people of color, especially those with HIV/AIDS. But as the riot spread and fire trucks raced past, Jewel knew it was time to go. She packed up her two dogs and her parrot, called her life partner Rue to come get her, and called an employee who lives in the area to say she was leaving. At age fifty-three, Jewel had withstood racism, sexism, homophobia, financial fluctuations, the rocky road back from drug and alcohol abuse, and the loss of close friends. But surrendering her prized business to fate was one of the hardest things she had ever had to do.

What Jewel and Rue didn't discover until early the next morning, was that the Catch's gay and straight neighbors, led by two "fearless lesbians," kicked out knife-wielding looters and saved the disco from being torched. They also learned that Rue's House—the nation's first shelter for women and children with AIDS that they had founded together in April 1989—had come through unscathed. In both cases Jewel and Rue were told that their friends and neighbors had protected them because of all they had given to the community. "My idea of a panacea for all our ills is being of service," says Jewel. "And ironically, by being of service, Rue and I have even greater happiness in our own relationship."

Jewel and Rue have been able to make their way together in both the heterosexual and homosexual worlds. I just think they're an inspiration to everyone.

—Maxine Waters
U.S. CONGRESSWOMAN

Written by Laura M. Markowitz

JoAnn Loulan

LESBIAN SEX EDUCATOR, WRITER AND THERAPIST

You younger generation of lesbians have a much freer attitude about sex. I like to say that we worked our fingers to the bone—literally!—so you wouldn't have to suffer like we did.

The cover of JoAnn Loulan's first book is hot pink, with the words *Lesbian Sex* pulsating off the spine. Loulan, author of this ground-breaking mind-opening how-to manual for lesbians, laughs mischievously, "I wanted to blare *Lesbian Sex* in every lesbian living room around the country, loud and proud. My message is that we deserve great sex!"

A psychotherapist and sex educator in California's Portola Valley, Loulan began her teaching career lecturing about lesbian culture and sexuality to a class of doctors and medical students at the University of California in San Francisco. During one session she described alternative insemination, which she herself later used to have her son in 1982. After the class, a female gynecologist approached Loulan and asked, "So what exactly is a lesbian mother?" A light bulb went off. "This woman couldn't even wrap her mind around the two words together—*lesbian and mother,*" says Loulan. "I realized I needed to redouble my efforts to eradicate homophobia."

These days, when Loulan speaks in front of an audience, it is part comedy routine, part therapy, and part physiology lesson. "My mission is to define woman-to-woman mores, rules, and sexual action," she says. "Our ability to do this is impacted by our varied gender identities. The concept that there are only two genders is not only absurd, it has thwarted lesbian sexual development. My book in progress, *Gender Jail*, suggests that in order to bust loose from the old constraints, we need to invent language that describes our many and unique genders. This will set us free."

Loulan has sold more than fifty thousand copies of *Lesbian Sex,* and more that two hundred thousand copies of her other *books, The Lesbian Erotic Dance: Butch, Femme, Androgyny and Other Rhythms; Lesbian Passion: Loving Ourselves and Each Other;* and *Period.* "I want lesbians to love lesbianism," she says, "and that includes having and liking sex." She has coached a generation of lesbians not to wait for a romanticized, Hollywood notion to propel them into bed. "I'm a big believer in getting conscious about sex and saying what it is you want—asking for it and talking about it out loud. At first, a lot of lesbians were mad at me for being so outspoken, and afraid of what the straight community, and even the lesbian community, would say. Now they seem to revel in my message: Sex is a way for lesbians to experience love and excitement, while at the same time nurturing our movement."

Loulan is the Eisenhower of lesbian sex. She looks like such a nice girl and says the most outrageous things.

—Susie Bright
SEXPERT

194

Bob and Rod Jackson-Paris

FOUNDERS OF THE BE TRUE TO YOURSELF FOUNDATION

We received a letter from a fifteen-year-old boy who wrote that he had recently asked his guidance counselor what he thought about gay people. The counselor responded, 'I think they should all kill themselves.' So the boy planned his suicide, and wrote that he had the means and was going to do it the next day.

When a gay teenager wrote to human rights activists Bob and Rod-Jackson Paris and talked of suicide, their hearts sank. But the couple read on and discovered that the boy's letter was not a suicide note at all—he had concluded by saying that after seeing the two of them on *Oprah,* for the first time in his life, he felt he could simply be himself—the person he was meant to be. The Jackson-Parises had inspired him to cancel his suicide plans.

The couple's appearances on *Oprah, Donahue,* and other television programs have generated many similar letters from gay and lesbian youths. These letters in turn sparked the video *Be True To Yourself,* in which the Jackson-Parises and ten teenagers discuss teen suicide, homophobia, self esteem, and coming out issues. They have since set out to create a fundraising mechanism for similar projects and support services for gay, lesbian, and bisexual youth, through the Be True To Yourself Foundation. Their autobiography, the national best-seller *Straight From the Heart,* not only tells their story, but serves as an implicit guide to coming out and learning to love.

Bob Paris, a former Mr. Universe, and Rod Jackson, an international model, met at a gym in Denver, Colorado in 1985. Four years later they were married. Because the couple feels that marriage is the highest form of commitment in our culture, it came naturally to declare their love for one another in a Unitarian Church. Together they offer a compelling example of love against the odds.

In February 1994, the Jackson-Parises were invited to the White House to meet the Clintons. They thanked President Clinton for a recent letter he had written decrying anti-gay ballot measures and chastising the religious right for attempting to legalize discrimination against gay men and lesbians. They continue to set an example as positive role models with their efforts in support of gay and lesbian civil rights by lecturing at colleges and appearing at fundraisers nationwide.

Bob and Rod are gay America's First Couple. They smash stereotypes wherever they appear, and speak eloquently for justice and equality. They are making sure the next generation of gay and lesbian youth will have their self-esteem firmly in place and won't suffer the consequences of ignorance and homophobia we have all suffered growing up.

—William Waybourne
GAY AND LESBIAN VICTORY FUND

195

Rob Eichberg, PhD

AUTHOR AND FOUNDER OF NATIONAL COMING OUT DAY

At the 1987 March on Washington, I asked people if they were out to their families, friends, and co-workers. Most weren't. We had six hundred thousand people marching who weren't getting support from their natural allies—the people in their own daily lives.

Rob Eichberg knew it was time somebody did something. He believed that the message of the 1987 March on Washington for Gay and Lesbian Rights would be lost if people did not come out of the closet. So he went home and started organizing with a determined passion—believing in the transformational power of telling the truth. One year later, October 11, 1988, marked the first annual National Coming Out Day. And just as Eichberg had hoped, the idea caught on. Television stars like Dick Sargent of *Bewitched* and Amanda Bearse of *Married...With Children* would publicly come out on later NCODs. Teachers would use it to spark discussions in schools across America. By 1993, NCOD was celebrated in forty-four states and three countries.

While Eichberg was working for a social-service agency in the mid-seventies in Los Angeles, he was jolted one day when several of his associates made homophobic remarks. At that moment, he realized that he had his own constituency in need of help. He helped create the Municipal Elections Committee of Los Angeles, the first gay and lesbian political action committee in the United States, and a model for the Human Rights Campaign Fund. But Eichberg recognized that personal growth precedes political activism, and he launched *The Experience* with the late David Goodstein. There are now over thirty thousand graduates of *The Experience* workshops.

"Our vision is that by the year 2000, it will be absolutely okay to be lesbian or gay," says Eichberg, "and that diversity will be valued and celebrated." Believing that remaining closeted is detrimental to personal growth and development, Eichberg remains committed to changing the way people feel about being gay. "Coming out is a continual process," he says. "Most lesbians and gays, as kids, know their survival would be threatened if they come out, so they decide to hide. A major component of *The Experience* is re-examining that decision to hide as adults. There is a lot of evidence that out of the closet, people do better in the workplace and in their personal lives, because they aren't wasting time and energy hiding. If there is a problem where you work, take your talents elsewhere. If your parents reject you, it is an opportunity to become a whole adult on your own. Even people who have had negative experiences coming out generally say they would do it again. The value of personal freedom and liberation is that great!"

Rob Eichberg is constantly coming up with ways to get people—gay or straight—to be more conscious, responsible, accepting, and loving. He is a wonderful example of self-esteem and purpose combined to create the kind of person the world badly needs.

—Judith Light
ACTRESS

JEB (Joan E. Biren)

PHOTOGRAPHER

The 1980s were years of increasing repression and then increasing resistance, years in which I held my camera and felt it to be a barometer measuring the pressure against us. When more and more lesbians chose to step in from of my lens, I knew the atmosphere had changed, and that we had changed it.

Holding a borrowed camera at arm's length, Joan E. Biren kissed her lover and snapped—taking her very first lesbian photograph. It was the early 1970s, and Biren didn't know any other women who would allow themselves to be photographed kissing. Since then, through her extraordinary images, she has "given the movement a face," in the words of one writer. Indeed, Biren—better known as JEB—has documented the movement like no one else.

In the '70s, JEB's work appeared in *off our backs* and the feminist quarterly *Quest;* on record covers for Willie Tyson, Casse Culver and Meg Christian; and in many other places. But as she became involved with the poet Minnie Bruce Pratt in what would turn out to be an eleven-year relationship, JEB began to sense that she could be as much artist as photojournalist. "I began to understand much more about the creative process—watching Minnie Bruce's, talking about mine with her," JEB says. "That was profound, and very important to me. In a way, I was learning to respect my own work."

JEB broke new ground with her 1979 book *Eye to Eye: Portraits of Lesbians.* Here for the first time were women proudly naming themselves as lesbians, and standing forthrightly in front of the camera. In *Making a Way: Lesbians Out Front,* JEB captured for posterity the faces of famous activists and artists such as May Sarton, Audre Lorde, Stormé DeLarverié, Del Martin and Phyllis Lyon, and Urvashi Vaid, and everyday heroes like Abigail Johnson, who then ran a Christmas-tree farm in Georgia. JEB's books were passed from woman to woman all over the country, where they were treasured for their celebration of lesbians as people of all kinds, all colors, and all classes.

After *For Love and For Life,* her multimedia photo-documentary of the 1987 March on Washington, was transferred from slides to videotape and broadcast on public television, JEB began to imagine herself working in a new medium. She gave up the darkroom for the edit bay—and went on to open 1993's annual gay film festival in Washington with *A Simple Matter of Justice,* the official documentary video of the 1993 March on Washington for Lesbian, Gay and Bisexual Equal Rights. The video bears JEB's hallmarks like an activist's badge. *A Simple Matter of Justice* is about a committed people and their cause—a movement movingly documented. And that, after all, is what people think of when they hear JEB's name.

A lot of the way we as lesbians have come to know ourselves and feel good about ourselves has been through JEB's images. They provide an energy of self-acceptance that makes our struggle possible—that's the work of a cultural artist.

—Joan Nestle
FOUNDER, LESBIAN
HERSTORY ARCHIVE

Paul Cadmus

PAINTER

W. H. Auden wrote, '...we must love one another or die.' He then changed this to '...we must love one another and die.' Was the first injunction impossible to achieve? I think it is. I can't love everyone. I don't denigrate love. I've learned to respect the word respect. It is what is most important for daily living, for getting along with others. We must respect one another, no matter what shade, what shape, what orientation. Beyond this, I fail. I cannot tolerate intolerance.

Paul Cadmus stood amid an assembly of art-world celebrities at Manhattan's Museum of Modern Art. It was November 1984 and Cadmus had been out of the limelight for four decades. Shockingly, MOMA displays none of the New York-born artist's work, but this night the film department of the museum was hosting a glittering celebration of him on film, *Paul Cadmus: Enfant Terrible at 80*.

Cadmus' painting began getting attention in 1934 with *The Fleet's In*, his vision of servicemen on leave with dates both male and female—the first of several meticulously crafted, classically disciplined, and socially biting works to win international notoriety and the wrath of self-styled patriots. The craft and intelligence of his paintings made their satire of moral and political hypocrisy stand out in the social-realist 1930s. By the early 1940s, though, an art world mad for modernism rejected his Florentine craftsmanship; a country tooling up for war rejected his criticism; and a culture steeped in Puritanism rejected his adoring emphasis on male beauty. He was ostracized by consensus, but was supported for forty years by the loyal Midtown Gallery, the Whitney Museum and discerning patrons—especially for his unparalleled drawings of male nudes posed for by his lover, the singer Jon Andersson.

Yet with time, modernism's power over the public eroded, the 1960s brought wide-spread condemnation of hypocrisy, and those in the gay rights movement demanded to know their heroes and history. In 1975, Cadmus was elected to the American Academy of Arts and Letters, and museums began dusting his work off for display. New fans joined the old. In 1984, Lincoln Kirsten published a lavish book about the man and his work, and Cadmus found himself honored in the very temple of modernity, the Museum of Modern Art.

Cadmus stood there that night among flashbulbs and handshakes, observing the praise and adulation of his "revival" with the same clear critical eye he brought to his first brush with fame, and to the long years of dignified exile. In one sense, nothing had changed. Cadmus had never stopped producing solid and individual masterpieces, some of the most important works of modern American art.

For Cadmus, man's error lies not in his being human, but in his being less than what being human could and should entail. The pure joy that emanates from a Cadmus drawing of a human being is what reveals the essential core of his view of his fellow man.

—Raymond J. Steiner

ART TIMES

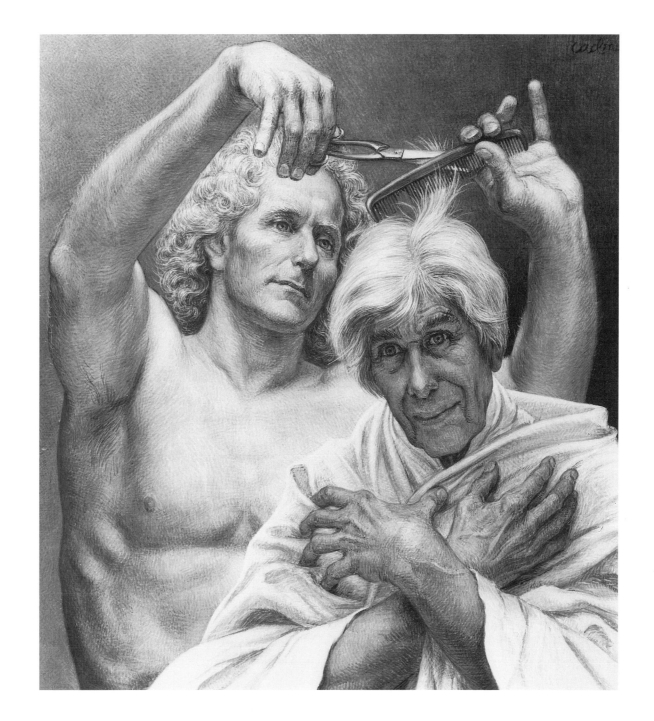

Photographed by Reginald Pearman
Courtesy Olivia Records

Written by Joelle Yuna

Judy Dlugacz

OLIVIA RECORDS AND OLIVIA TRAVEL PRESIDENT

Twenty years ago we had a vision that spoke of changing the world. We believed that lesbianism was not only a lifestyle, but an incredibly positive choice women could make in their lives, to change their lives, to liberate their lives.

With four other young women, Judy Dlugacz borrowed $4,000 in 1973 and started Olivia Records, believing it could thrive using only women musicians, technicians, distributors, and concert producers. Over the years, as members of the company left to fulfill other dreams, Dlugacz stayed on, nurturing the music and the artists—among them Cris Williamson, Meg Christian, Tret Fure, Teresa Trull, Lucie Blue Tremblay, and Deidre McCalla. Olivia Records came to seem like a personal friend and role model to lesbians everywhere, giving words and music to dreams and unspoken thoughts, creating a place to meet, and to be whole. The music became a means of both recognition and visibility.

Through Dlugacz's leadership, Olivia has produced over forty records and made possible thousands of concerts around the world. In 1990 Dlugacz diversified her business and created Olivia Travel, offering cruises and vacations for women that were never before possible, and in 1993 she began managing the career of Suzanne Westenhoefer, one of the fastest rising stars in comedy.

It is Dlugacz's personal dedication, her absolute unwillingness to give up—even when the cupboard is bare—that has allowed her to give the gift of pride and visibility to so many lesbians all over the world. But ask her what she has done, and she'll turn it around and express her thanks to the women who have supported Olivia over the years. At the company's twentieth anniversary celebration in 1993, Dlugacz said to the standing-room only audience, "Do not for one minute underestimate the part we all played in changing this world. For we are the ones who first opened the closet doors as lesbians and feminists. We are the ones who created the bridge—by seeing the immense possibility of our own lives. And so, when we applaud these accomplishments, we must applaud the immense task we all took on—and the extraordinary results created by the first generation to rise up en masse and change the world forever for women and lesbians and gays."

In a time dominated by politics often unsympathetic to women in general, and lesbians in particular, Judy Dlugacz has stood on the front lines, demanding for all of us the right to be simply, exactly, who we are. In a world of music, she's the unsung heroine.

—Carole Migden
SAN FRANCISCO
SUPERVISOR

203

Richard Burns

EXECUTIVE DIRECTOR, LESBIAN AND GAY COMMUNITY SERVICES CENTER, NEW YORK

Anita Bryant, the '79 March, the '87 March, the military issue—everything is an organizing tool. Each time we have to defend ourselves as a community, more people come out of the closet, take risks, perform acts of courage, give money, and write letters. I think that when we go through one of these processes, we emerge stronger because our numbers become greater.

Richard Burns was always a gay activist. At age twenty-two, fresh out of college, he moved to Boston expressly to work as a volunteer for the *Gay Community News*. He went on to become a staff member in January 1978, and eventually, managing editor. *GCN* was then the only lesbian and gay newsweekly in the United States.

"That was an incredibly exciting time for me," says Burns. "I was exposed to and immersed in so many issues critical to the changing world of lesbian and gay liberation in the decade following Stonewall." It was during those years at *GCN* that he grew to understand the connections between various struggles for justice, between reproductive freedom and lesbian and gay freedom, and to make the essential connections between the fight for lesbian and gay liberation, feminism, and the fight against racism. "Through the power of that newspaper," he says, "working very specifically to get the word out on community organizing, we were able to be a part of a larger national struggle."

In the late 1970s, localized lesbian and gay civil rights efforts were organized in isolation across the country, and there was no truly national gay and lesbian movement. But the power of a national gay news weekly, the way it facilitated cross-pollination and the exchange of vital information between local gay liberation movements, impressed upon Burns the power of a newspaper as a national organizing tool. "It's the same way I think about the Lesbian and Gay Community Services Center today," he says. "It exists to facilitate organizing and to build community."

Richard is one of the smartest, most dedicated and creative organizers in the national gay and lesbian liberation movement. He has a broad political vision, and has worked for nearly twenty years to build inclusive organizations that represent the diversity of our people. I admire his energy and integrity, and love his faith in the basic decency and goodness of gay and lesbian people.

—Urvashi Vaid
ATTORNEY AND POLITICAL ANALYST

Photographed by David Martin
Courtesy New York Lesbian and Gay Community Services Center

Written by Jane DeLynn

Sharon Kowalski and Karen Thompson

ACTIVISTS

I became an activist by accident. I stood up for Sharon's rights, and as a result began to make connections to issues far bigger than the two of us—not just homophobia, but sexism, ableism, and heterosexism. There's no such thing as a passive anti-oppressor. If I don't stand up for someone's rights today, tomorrow I could lose mine. –Karen Thompson

In 1984, when Karen Thompson decided to sue for legal guardianship of her lover, Sharon Kowalski, who had become paralyzed and unable to talk following an automobile crash, it meant having to admit publicly that she was a lesbian. Thus began the transformation of a closeted Reaganite Republican into virtually a full-time activist and speaker. The fight she embarked on took longer than anyone could have imagined. It wasn't until April 1993, almost ten years after Kowalski's accident, after legal expenditures of over $225,000 and court battles that ranged all the way up to the Supreme Court, that Kowalski was finally allowed to come home to the wheelchair-accessible house that Thompson had built for her.

For three and a half years of that time, the two were prevented from seeing each other by Kowalski's father. But Thompson never forgot what Kowalski had painstakingly typed out for her the last time she had seen her; "Help me, take me home with you." When the court finally ruled in Thompson's—and Kowalski's—favor, it was the first guardianship case in the nation in which an appeals court recognized a homosexual partner's rights as tantamount to that of a spouse. Civil rights activists consider the case to be the most important legal victory for the rights of the disabled, gay or straight, ever to occur in this country.

"I've learned that as long as we're invisible, we're vulnerable," says Thompson. "Nothing has happened to me out of the closet that was anywhere near as dangerous as being closeted. I'm happier than I ever dared would be possible again. Every day is hard work, but I've never asked that things be easy, just that they be possible."

Through your action and your impassioned speeches, you have caused the American public, law makers, and people in the medical profession to take note of the importance of caregiving of persons by those who love them.

–THE NATIONAL
CONFERENCE
FOR COLLEGE WOMEN
STUDENT LEADERS

AFTER PRESENTING
THE *WOMEN OF
DISTINCTION 1993*
AWARD TO
KAREN THOMPSON

Dr. Tom Waddell

GAY GAMES FOUNDER AND OLYMPIC ATHLETE
Well this should be interesting. —Dr. Tom Waddell's final words

He may be the most impressive human being I ever met. Certainly he was the most impressive athlete. He combined strength and sensitivity, intelligence and courage, compassion and competitiveness, in dazzling doses. He contradicted all the stereotypes of both the athlete and the homosexual.

—Dick Schapp
ABC NEWS

For the opening ceremonies of the first meet of the Gay Games in 1982, an apprehensive group of athletes had joined together on a cloudy, dreary San Francisco day. Dr. Tom Waddell, the man whose vision and energy made the Games possible, stepped up to the microphone and quietly said, "Let it shine." Minutes later the whole stadium was chanting with him, "Let it shine!" Soon the sun came out. And the Games began. Whether on the sun or the spirit of the crowd, the magic of Waddell had worked again.

Waddell conceived the Gay Games as an athletic festival to foster both gay pride and the Olympic ideal of excellence. He wanted to "educate people through sport in a spirit of better understanding" and believed the Games would shatter stereotypes of gay men being unathletic, as well as dignify and motivate gay athletes. He also hoped to bridge the long-standing gap between gay men and women. This was particularly important to him because in addition to having many women friends, he had married an athlete, Sara Lewintein, whom he met at the Games. They conceived a daughter, Jessica, born in 1983.

Tom Waddell was many things to many people: College football player, gymnast (competing for Springfield College, he once out-scored the entire Amherst team), and decathlete on the Olympic team at thirty, finishing sixth in the 1968 Olympics in Mexico City. He was a U.S. Army doctor, though morally opposed to the Vietnam War, and went on to specialize in infectious diseases. Waddell also has the distinction of being one-half of the first gay couple ever featured in *People*.

Surrounded by his many friends and his wife, Waddell died of AIDS in 1987 at the age of forty-nine. Today his legacy lives on in his beloved Gay Games, which are the fastest-growing international sporting and cultural event in the world.

Lea DeLaria

COMEDIAN

I want Martina Navratilova to strap on her tennis racket and take me from behind like the dog that I am.

At the 1993 March on Washington, Lea DeLaria knew why she was there, and what she was fighting for. "I'm demanding the right for a date," she said. "I thought it was really nice of them to get this march together so that I could get a date. When I look out at this, all of the girls are so gorgeous. I look at it this way: if I were locked in a pastry store overnight in Paris, and someone came up to me and said I could eat everything I want and not gain any weight, that's how I feel about this march—fabulous!"

If DeLaria is still looking for a date, it's probably the only thing that hasn't been going her way. She hosted Comedy Central's *Out There,* the first national all gay and lesbian comedy special, and with appearances on *Matlock, The John Larroquette Show, 20/20,* and *The Arsenio Hall Show,* her career has been blossoming. As an openly lesbian comic, she has gotten the straight world to laugh with her, not at her. "I want the right to be visible," she says, "so that people throughout the country can see what a lesbian looks like. We're not going to bite you. We're not going to steal your children—well maybe Chelsea."

It isn't hard for DeLaria to remember what it was like to be in high school, to be coming to terms with being different. "My best friend in school was gay," she says. "When he walked down the hall his feet didn't touch the floor. We're talking gay boy! But he never said anything about it. I'd stand up for him and say, 'He's not a fag! Leave him alone!' And in my head I'm thinking, 'Please God, don't let them find out I'm a dyke.' Terrified! We were the closest of friends and he finally told me on graduation day, 'You have to stop telling people I'm not a fag, because I am one.' And I said, 'Well, God, so am I.' It was such a relief. If we can all be more visible, then a lot of kids out there could feel better."

Doing a soundbite seems so phony, 'Lea DeLaria is la-la-la. She's a human super nova.' And Lea'd say to me, 'Oh Scott really, who are you trying to kid?' Actually, I have a lot of affection for her. She is an accomplished jazz singer and a talented actor. What you see with Lea is what you get. She has so much energy, she makes me tired.

—Scott Thompson
COMIC, THE KIDS
IN THE HALL

Tee Corinne

VISUAL ARTIST, EDITOR AND WRITER

Sexuality is what people keep wanting to clean up and pretend doesn't happen—desexualize lesbians and make them okay. But sexuality is a defining bottom line: if we are not sexual then a lot of the persecution that has happened to lesbians—the fact of it—just disappears. I mean, we're persecuted because we're sexual, not because we're nice little old ladies who like other women.

Tee Corinne is no stranger to the subversiveness of lesbian sexual imagery, both written and visual, whether in her own work or that of the diverse sensibilities she assembles. "In most of the U.S. and the world," she says, "lesbian sexuality is still censored and often illegal. Writing erotica is a radical and extremely political act." Corinne is a veritable lesbian feminist institution, best known as the editor of erotica collections such as *The Body of Love; Riding Desire;* the Lambda Literary Award-winner *Intricate Passions;* and *The Poetry of Sex: Lesbians Write the Erotic.*

Long before lesbian erotica was hot, at a time when lesbians were still uncertain about how to deal with the *sex* in their homosexuality, Corinne self-published a little book of explicit line drawings called *The Cunt Coloring Book,* and began one of her life missions. Her graphic depictions of women of all shapes, sizes, beauties and physical abilities have departed from both fashionable standards of sexual correctness and from the *Playboy* mentality.

Corinne's interest in using sexual imagery in her work first became apparent in the 1970s when, after receiving an MFA from the Pratt Institute, she moved to the Bay Area and worked as a sex educator for the San Francisco Sex Information Switchboard. She credits "that wild and inclusive" community with helping influence the creation of the *Coloring Book* and her later fiction, *Dreams of the Woman Who Loved Sex; Lovers: Love and Sex Stories* (recently banned in Canada); and *The Sparkling Lavender Dust of Lust.* In 1977, one of a series of her photographs became the renowned cover for the feminist journal *Sinister Wisdom,* and was later printed as a poster. "The further away we get from the erotic," she says, "the more power we lose. Take away the sex and we're not objectionable at all."

But her life isn't just about sex: she has done over three hundred portraits of women writers, was Naiad Press' first main cover artist, started a gay and lesbian caucus within the College Art Association, founded *The Blatant Image/A Magazine of Feminist Photography,* and has contributed as an artist, editor, writer, and critic to countless publications and exhibits. An expatriate Southerner now living in Oregon where she teaches, Corinne continues to push the bounds of who nice girls are and what nice girls do.

There is still a very narrow perception of what lesbian sexuality is. Tee Corinne has made a tremendous effort to have a range of deeply sensual images—women of color, disabled women, older women—images we would not see otherwise. That is what is so powerful about her work.

—Victoria Brownworth
THE ADVOCATE

Nicole Ramirez Murray

STONEWALL 25 CO-CHAIR

Around the time of Stonewall, the police in San Diego, California were beating up gays. I organized demonstrations. So the police tried to run me out of town. I was arrested three times in one day for being in female attire. They even arrested me for throwing cigarette ashes on the street. I've never smoked in my life.

Nicole has lead the fight to benefit those in need, to protect civil rights, celebrate achievement, and to further the interests of the gay and lesbian community and also the Latino community. Therefore, I declare December 3, 1987 'Nicole Ramirez Murray Day.'

—Maureen O'Connor
SAN DIEGO MAYOR

President Clinton walked up and introduced himself to Nicole Ramirez Murray at a campaign function in 1992. "When he saw my red ribbon," says Murray, "he looked into my eyes and said 'AIDS has touched me too.' I think he was thinking of someone he knew because I saw sadness in his eyes. Later, when I posed for a photograph with him, Clinton asked me to repeat my name. I replied 'Nicole,' he smiled and said, 'Oh, I see!'" Murray doesn't hide being a drag queen, no matter where he is. "In my closet, on one side I have suits and ties," he says. "On the other side, I have gowns and crowns. I know when to wear a dress and when to wear a suit."

Playing his different roles, Murray serves the community with style and grace, whether as the first chairman of the City of San Diego's Gay and Lesbian Advisory Board, executive board member of the Human Rights Campaign Fund, founder of three AIDS organizations, or as the six-time Empress of San Diego's Imperial Court. "People have forgotten the role of drag queens," he says. "We have a long history of activism. Thirty years ago, we were the only fund-raising vehicle for the gay and lesbian community."

Murray's activism even extends into Mexico, where he has seen people with AIDS living in cardboard houses. In 1989, he received a call from a gay activist in Tijuana. The man told him that the morticians wouldn't handle the bodies of those who had died from AIDS. He asked Murray, "Please help us. We need body bags to bury our dead and have no place to get them." Murray raised the money for body bags. No fuss—just an endless capacity for getting things done. San Diego's gay and lesbian community still supplies those body bags.

A tireless fundraiser for political candidates, gay and lesbian rights activists, battered women, abused children, lesbian health care providers, and AIDS service organizations; in 1994 Murray received the first annual Caesar E. Chavez Justice Award, presented by Chavez' widow for "twenty years of striving for social justice and giving of oneself to others in need." Murray even supports the police department that once arrested him for allegedly throwing ashes in the street, and it was because of his efforts that when a memorial to San Diego Police officers who died in the line of duty was dedicated, the police chief cited two major contributors: the Boy Scouts and the gay and lesbian community.

214

215

Photographed by John R. Selig

Michelangelo Signorile

WRITER AND ACTIVIST

If you print the truth, you are deemed frightening and offensive. When straight people's sex lives are written about, it's considered 'news' in every publication from People to the New York Times, but if gay people's sex lives are written about, it's an 'infringement of privacy.' Well, I call it homophobia—from both straight people and gay people alike.

When Larry Kramer called Michelangelo Signorile's *Queer in America* "one of the most important books of the twentieth century," he was declaring the book, published in 1993, and the phenomena of theory and activism it represented, to be a milestone in the histories of homosexuality, journalism, and the twentieth century—and his assessment of Signorile's seismic impact does not stand alone. Larry Gross comes to the same conclusion in *Contested Closets: the Politics and Ethics of Outing,* the most scholarly and exhaustive study of outing yet published.

Signorile began making a journalistic splash in 1989, when his "Gossip Watch" column for *OutWeek* magazine signaled the end of the "Execrable Eighties." He had started as a "planter" for the mainstream gossip columnists he would later expose for their double standards. "It was so corrupt," he says, and credits the dishonesty of the gossip world, particularly as it relates to gay men and lesbians, with planting the seed of his own anger at the media, and spurring his involvement in ACT UP. Signorile was soon a leading activist of the queer generation and one of the most controversial journalists ever; the relatively few times he outed celebrities and public figures drew intense international media coverage and sparked furious debate throughout both the straight and gay communities.

In Spring 1992, *The Advocate* published Signorile's two-part investigation, "Out at the *New York Times.*" Many pundits felt it was one of the most important features ever to appear in the gay press: The *Times,* long believed to be one of the premiere obstacles to balanced perceptions in the media about the lives of lesbians and gay men, had finally been explored fully—the failure of some of its AIDS coverage, the hypocrisy of its own closeted reporters and the homophobia of former editor-in-chief Abe Rosenthal—revealed in rich detail. Signorile concluded his story on the *Times* with an ebullient description of a joint Christmas party of the Publishing Triangle (an association of gay and lesbian writers, editors and publishers), and the New York chapter of the Lesbian and Gay Journalists Association. "This was all very new, and power was what everyone was getting off on," Signorile said, "the extraordinary collective power that we all realized could be harnessed if we worked together."

What Signorile is saying is that if being gay is not disgusting, is not awful, then why can't we talk about it? After all, it's not an insult to call someone gay. Is it?

—Vito Russo
THE CELLULOID CLOSET

Photographed by Jerome Friar/Impact Visuals

Written by Mark Chesnut

Ann Northrop

ACTIVIST AND JOURNALIST

Activists embody the highest standard of values. They set the standards in some way, and then the inside people try to reach a compromise. In the Paul Revere tradition, activists alert the populace about what needs to be changed by going out into the streets and yelling. I don't think any one strategy can succeed; a complex arsenal is necessary to any movement.

Approaching her fifth year as a producer at the *CBS Morning News* in 1986, Ann Northrop tired of the constant pressure and was ready to make some changes. "I was fed up with working too hard, and not having time for my lover and her two kids," she says. "I thought there had to be a way for me to be happier in life." Walking away from her high-paying career in broadcast journalism took guts. So did choosing an uncertain future educating the straight community about AIDS and gay and lesbian rights.

When Northrop left CBS she had no clear path in mind, but knew she wanted to combine her chief interests: sports, young people, and serving the gay and lesbian community. Thinking she might become some kind of coach, she interviewed at the Harvey Milk School in Manhattan, a school for gay and lesbian youth, and was told they didn't have a gym. But they did have an opening for a public speaker dealing with AIDS education. "You mean you want to pay me cash money to speak in public?" Northrop had asked. "Sign me up!" She was very enthusiastic, but had some concerns, wondering if "ghettoizing" herself might mean committing professional suicide. But she took the risk—and it paid off, giving her a sense of satisfaction and increased awareness. "I had no dedication to AIDS issues before I quit CBS," she says. "But when I went to Harvey Milk, it took about six seconds to become revolutionized."

The next step of her involvement in the gay and lesbian community came during a 1988 visit to an ACT UP meeting, where Northrop saw the same brand of street activism she had known in both the women's and anti-war movements. "It was exactly what I was looking for," she says. "Part of it was my nostalgia for the sixties, but ACT UP embodies my values. I like to get out on the streets, march around and yell slogans. I like to confront bad situations and demand change."

Northrop was also a columnist for *QW* magazine and is a board member of Gay Games IV. She feels that her activism boils down to a concern for other people. "There are two schools of thought in the world," she says. "One is survival of the fittest. The second school of thought says the only way we can survive is if we take care of each other. Well, every time I let something go by that is bigoted or rotten, I feel lousy. If you don't fight this stuff, what's the point?"

Wherever Ann goes there is a rush of energy and ideas. She then leads us through the whirlwind with great clarity and principle.

—Ronnie Eldridge
NEW YORK CITY
COUNCILMEMBER

Garrett Glaser

TELEVISION REPORTER

Every so often I do think about the fact that I'm making history. I think about it in bits and pieces, when I'm about to go to sleep and am trying to put my day in context. I understand how important it is that I acknowledge what I do. But I get afraid that if I say it too loud, I'll lose a certain drive to go farther with all of this. Yet I often wish that as a movement we could take more notice of our accomplishments. I was at Stonewall the night after the first riot, back when gay clubs and bars had little peepholes where they would look at you before they let you in. How far we've come in two and a half decades. It's so important that we let that sink in.

Garrett Glaser was standing before a thousand people at the 1992 convention of the Radio and Television News Directors Association in San Antonio. In his seventeen-year career in journalism he had never pretended to be something he wasn't. But this was different. Glaser was speaking as an openly gay man at a panel on diversity in the newsroom. Many in the audience were former colleagues; some were former (and future) bosses. In fact, just about every news director in America was there. It was a big step in what Glaser sees as a series of small ones.

In 1990, when he began working as a volunteer for the Gay and Lesbian Alliance Against Defamation, he was open but not public about his sexual orientation. A year later GLAAD asked him to run for the board. He knew that his name would then be on the newsletter that was sent to ten thousand people every month, including his executive producer at *Entertainment Tonight*. "I knew a lot of people in the industry would see my name and go, 'Oh, so this guy is gay and *out!*' But I knew it wasn't healthy for me to be closeted in any way," he says. "And the people at *ET* were great about it. If you think enough of yourself to be open and honest in every way about who you are, people can't help but respond. I have never regretted the decision to be out. Never."

Glaser is one of only a handful of openly gay or lesbian television personalities in America. He has gone on to host two episodes of the acclaimed PBS series on gay men and lesbians, *In the Life*, and is strenuously lobbying cable and broadcast networks to start a gay television channel.

"It's all about creating positive role models," he says. "It's amazing how resilient and successful we are as a community considering how we are brought up to feel about ourselves. How is it that we are so loving after the way we have been conditioned? After some of us have been thrown out on the street or almost beaten to death? It's a miracle. We are blessed. But think of how great it would be if gay kids could see people on television, and see that it's okay to be comfortable with who they are. Just think of *that*."

Often, gay and lesbian youth are told that their sexuality will impede their success in the working world. Garrett is there to prove otherwise. I applaud him for being honest about himself, and not pretending to be something he is not.

—Leeza Gibbons
ENTERTAINMENT TONIGHT

Gus Van Sant

DIRECTOR AND SCREENWRITER

The best thing about being a gay artist is you get to meet other gay artists and go hang out.

Hollywood doesn't usually explore the lives of the kinds of characters Gus Van Sant creates: junkies, male prostitutes, working-class loners. Focusing on his own visions of humanity, Van Sant doesn't make judgments; he observes, letting his characters come to life. His debut film, *Mala Noche,* a wrenching tale of unrequited gay love, first brought him to the attention of American film critics and art-house audiences. *Drugstore Cowboy* followed, a serio-comic saga of addicts who rob pharmacies. Then in *My Own Private Idaho,* Van Sant captured what was arguably the finest performance in the tragically short career of actor River Phoenix, who played a narcoleptic gay hustler in love with Keanu Reeves.

Born in Louisville, Kentucky, Van Sant moved with his family to Portland, Oregon while still in his teens. The Northwest remains a tangible presence in much of his work, from its cloudy weather to the gay pick-up spots of Portland. He studied painting and film at the Rhode Island School of Design, but it was the work of Stanley Kubrick that ultimately led him to choose a path in cinema. Influenced artistically by what he calls the "Three Bs,"–Samuel Beckett, William S. Burroughs and The Beatles–Van Sant has always been drawn to subject matter that takes him far from his comfortable upbringing. He looks for distance from "regular life," seeking territories to get lost in. "Instead of outer space, it's the streets, or it's a drug den," he says.

A musician and rock video director as well as a film-maker, Van Sant has taken on the film version of Tom Robbins' comic fantasy *Even Cowgirls Get the Blues,* his first project to feature female characters predominantly. The film gives him a chance to spoof what he calls "righteousness about beliefs." His contemporary spin on Robbins' book involves the assertion that "political correctness is dangerous, and just another form of bigotry." Though unafraid to feature gay characters and themes, Van Sant has never regarded himself as an activist. Rather, he prefers the other-worldly, which he conjures in cinematic evocations of characters' dreams and hallucinations. "Nonsense makes more sense," he says, in the closest thing to an encapsulation of his creative philosophy as he is probably ever likely to provide.

Van Sant's vision of things as they are has a startling lucidity–a purity that transcends banal naturalism. He gives the most abject people and places a kind of integrity; harsh circumstances and desperate needs take on comic grace.

–David Ansen
NEWSWEEK

June Chan and Mariana Romo-Carmona

ACTIVISTS

My mother refers to Mariana as a 'good daughter.' —June Chan
My mother says she 'values and respects June.' —Mariana Romo-Carmona

A couple for over ten years, June Chan and Mariana Romo-Carmona work hard to create understanding among diverse peoples, starting at home with their own families. Romo-Carmona is Chilean and Chan is Chinese. Romo-Carmona fought unsuccessfully for custody of her son Christian for many years. Finally, when old enough to decide for himself, he came to live with Chan and Romo-Carmona. Today, Chan teaches Chris New York City street smarts and he teaches her how to play Nintendo.

Romo-Carmona's poetry and fiction has appeared in several of the lesbian and gay publications she has edited, including the issue of the *Portable Lower East Side* that attracted the attention of Jesse Helms and others in the right-wing movement who attacked the National Endowment for the Arts. When Pat Buchanan called the book "blasphemous" and "filthy," Romo-Carmona believes their attacks added to activists' credibility in airing the injustices of racism, classism, and sexism.

Chan's writing takes a different turn: *Ultrastructural Localization of Phenolethanolamine N-Methyl Transference in Sensory and Motor Nuclei of the Vagus Nerve* is but one of more than a dozen published papers she has co-authored over the last twelve years. Both women are intensely interested in documenting lesbian history. Romo-Carmona was an editor of the 1987 work *Compañeras: Latina Lesbians* which documents the existence and history of contemporary Latin-American Lesbians, and Chan has created a slide-show, *Asian Lesbians Past and Present*, that she has presented to conferences in Europe and the Americas. "As Asian lesbians, we desperately need to understand that we are not alone," says Chan. "Especially in the parts of the world where we are not part of the dominant culture." Romo-Carmona agrees. "I've had Latina women tell me that *Compañeras* has changed their lives," she says. "That it has set them free."

When *Miss Saigon* came to New York they were both actively involved in mobilizing the response. The Lambda Legal Defense Fund had planned a fundraiser around the play. "It presents racist and sexist images of Asian women, including the idea that Asian women will kill themselves for a white man," says Chan. "This was pointed out to Lambda Legal Defense Fund, but they refused to cancel their event," says Romo-Carmona. "So, I resigned my job there." Massive demonstrations by gay and lesbian communities and Asian/Pacific Islander communities ensued. "While we didn't like airing our dirty laundry in public," Romo-Carmona and Chan say, "We caused many organizations to recognize the importance of taking an anti-racist stance in their work."

Mariana and June are an international power couple, a local national treasure, New York's most hospitable hosts and Nintendo champs to boot.

—Penny Perkins
WRITER

224

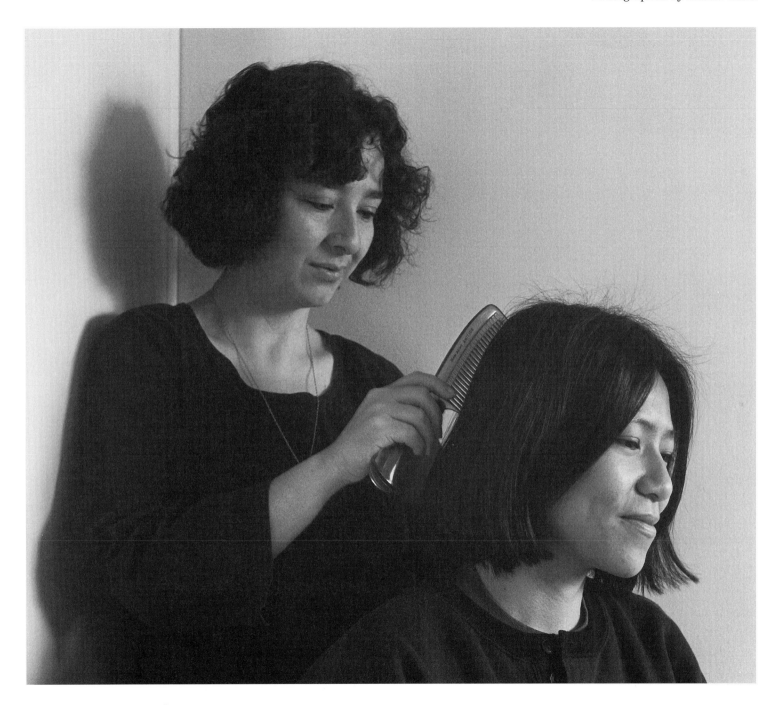

Michael Callen

SINGER AND AIDS ACTIVIST

Like some rabid animal, AIDS picked me up by the scruff of my neck, shook me senseless, and spat me out forever changed. I am today a totally different person than I was when the decade and epidemic began. AIDS has been a cosmic kick in the ass, a challenge to finally begin living fully.

Drowning in Kaposi's Sarcoma of the lungs, AIDS diva Michael Callen got himself on a plane to sing in front of nearly one million queers at the 1993 March on Washington. "Being gay is the greatest gift I ever had," Callen said before singing *Love Don't Need a Reason,* his gay-positive anthem. Never one to miss an opportunity for a witticism or to proclaim his feminism, Callen admitted to having a "wide-on" from singing in front of "so many of my ever-so-gay and lesbian people."

A self-described "AIDS Hope Pope" and "Pre-Madonna," Callen lived with unremitting attention to what he saw as his gay values. It made him friends—and enemies. He was an AIDS activist before there was an AIDS movement, one of the first to suggest that unprotected sex was making gay men sick. He helped create the entire concept of "safer sex." As a co-founder of the People With AIDS Coalition, the Community Research Initiative and the PWA Health Group, he called for "radical doubt" when it came to AIDS science and medications. "If I saw a friend about to drink a glass of Drano, I would knock it from his hand," he said in his 1990 book *Surviving AIDS.* "I consider AZT to be Drano in pill form."

Callen's highest calling was ethics. He wrote extensively about what he saw as the reality behind AIDS—shame—and promoted the "safer sex, more intimate, second sexual revolution" as a way to exorcise gay men's ingrained self-hatred and body shame. He spoke about gay people's tortured relationships to families: "Any gay person who survives being invisible to the world long enough to create themselves, to me, is just heartbreaking." Such a call for renewed self-creation is what Callen attempted to set forward in his last musical effort before death, a forty-song four-CD set he called *Legacy,* made with the help of Holly Near and Cris Williamson.

Music magically brought together Callen's thousand faces—then he could rest. "I want to fertilize a fruit tree," he said. "I was a tart in life and want to be a tart in death. Apple or cherry. Preferably cherry since I lost mine so many times." On December 27, 1993, Callen died at the age of thirty-nine. With his death, an era died: the age of gay men who had lived through the sexual liberation of the 1970s and through AIDS diagnoses of the 1980s—synthesizing the lessons of both those historically compressed decades. Callen's singing voice and printed words remain, placing "radical doubt" on all that keeps gay men and lesbians from living fully.

Michael Callen was an angel—one of our movement's greatest heroes and teachers.

—Torie Osborn
ACTIVIST

227

Denise L. Eger

RABBI

I believe the power of personal transformation is as much a part of Torah as the five Books of Moses. We see that power when we are public and normal about who we are. And the more we identify our-selves as family through alternative and varied structures, the more we challenge who the mainstream thinks we are, then the more our personal power transforms how they think of us.

Rabbi Denise L. Eger and her partner Karen Siteman brought their newborn son Benjamin with them to the Pacific Area Reform Rabbis Conference in January 1994. As one of the first openly lesbian rabbis in America, Eger was conscious of the other rabbis watching her little family, and she knew how powerful that image was to them. Later at the event, a video of a recent lesbian wedding was shown. Afterwards, seventy-five percent of the rabbis at the conference said they would perform such a ceremony themselves or would consider it. Eger believes that putting a human face to the words *gay* and *lesbian* made a difference for those rabbis. It's part of what she calls the power of personal transformation.

While she was in rabbinical school at Hebrew Union College, many peers knew of her lesbianism, but if she had been publicly out she would have risked losing her chance to be ordained. Yet Jewish tradition honors truth. Where is the truth when one is forced to lie? After her ordination Rabbi Eger chose to go public. In 1990 the Central Conference of American Rabbis met to take up the issue of ordaining openly gay and lesbian rabbis; Eger decided to step forward, though it could have meant placing her career in jeopardy. She felt she had to put a human face to the issue. "I have no idea what life would have been like if I were not able to become a rabbi," she says. "A sense of sadness comes to mind, of not being able to fulfill a calling—a profound, nagging sense of loss. But refusing to allow gay men and lesbians to become rabbis forces them to lie, destroying their integrity and dignity, creating spiritual, emotional and sometimes even physical brokenness."

The conference voted to uphold the rights of gay men and lesbians to be ordained as rabbis, urging that all rabbis, regardless of sexual orientation, be accorded the opportunity to fulfill the sacred vocation which they have chosen. "All human beings are created *Betselem Elohim* (in the divine image)," read their report. "Their personhood must therefore be accorded full dignity. We endorse the view that all Jews are religiously equal and we are aware of loving and committed relationships between people of the same sex; so we call upon rabbis and congregations to treat with respect and to integrate fully all Jews into the life of the community." Rabbi Denise Eger, who serves Congregation Kol Ami in Los Angeles, couldn't have said it better herself.

Denise Eger's work gave mainstream religious Judaism its first look at an openly lesbian rabbi. She also gave many in the gay and lesbian community their first look at the Torah as a positive model for opening the Jewish faith to our community.

—Reverend Troy Perry
FOUNDER OF METROPOLITAN COMMUNITY CHURCHES

228

Harvey Fierstein

PLAYWRIGHT AND ACTOR

I remember members of the Mattachine Society saying that we had to look like heterosexuals—that in order to talk to the press we should look as normal as possible. We young ones yelled back, 'Fuck you! We are what we are!' In our own way, we were screaming, 'We're here, we're queer, get used to it!'

Harvey Fierstein is forever himself. His joy at winning two 1983 Tony Awards for Best Play *and* Best Actor in a leading role was real. So is his satisfaction at rising from Bensonhurst to eminence as the first commercially viable gay show-person.

He made his debut in drag at age sixteen in Andy Warhol's *PORK,* and, as a performer, gave his honey-gravel voice to the works of many first-generation, post-Stonewall gay playwrights. The first vehicle he wrote for himself, *In Search Of The Cobra Jewels,* was greeted by the *Village Voice* critic with, "First I was entertained, then I was frightened, then I didn't know where I was. What kind of theater is this?" That convinced Fierstein that he had a future in writing. He wrote two more drag musicals, *Freaky Pussy* and *Flatbush Tosca,* before beginning the trio of plays that would become *Torch Song Trilogy.* Three years and six theaters later, *Torch Song* finally reached Broadway for its epochal run of over one thousand performances. Fierstein followed this success with the book for *La Cage aux Folles* (which won him a third Tony), *Spookhouse,* and *Safe Sex.*

Fierstein has reached a point in his life where he can handle producers who dislike his flamboyance, coy talk-show hosts, comic imitators, and critics who attack from every side. He has moved comfortably into other media, acting in films like his own *Torch Song Trilogy, Garbo Talks, The Times of Harvey Milk,* and *Mrs. Doubtfire.* On television he was Rebecca's first love on *Cheers* (for which he received an Emmy nomination), and has been seen in *Murder She Wrote, The Simpson's,* and in his own HBO drama, *Tidy Endings.*

Fierstein's work represents gay people who demand and get love, respect, and success. The general audience's acceptance of his work has cleared the way for the once-unimaginable commercial popularity of other gay and lesbian writers and performers. "Heterosexuals are the ungrateful children of gay culture," says Fierstein. "They wear the clothes we design, live in our houses, listen to our music, learn from our literature, and dream of making love to us. It's time we were acknowledged."

Fierstein is a living, breathing theater all by himself.

— Jack Kroll
NEWSWEEK

Mary Renault

NOVELIST

I have never, for any reason, in any book of mine, falsified anything deliberately which I knew or believed to be true. One can at least desire the truth; and it is inconceivable to me how anyone deliberately betrays it.

Mary Challans was born in London in 1905, the daughter of a medical doctor, and was educated in Bristol and at St. Hugh's College Oxford. From childhood, Renault was determined to become a writer, but her parents were strongly opposed. After graduating she worked as a clerk for some years, living alone in one room, on a few pounds a week. Later, she trained at Oxford to be a registered nurse, where she met the woman with whom she would spend the rest of her life, Julie Mullard.

In 1939, using the pseudonym of Mary Renault, she published her first novel, Promise of Love, which touched on both male and female homosexuality. It was well-received in England and America, although some people thought it was shocking. Renault hoped she was now set for a career in writing, but with World War II, she was ordered back to full-time hospital nursing. It was not until 1948 when, together with Mullard, she immigrated to South Africa, and she discovered her true métier in the historical novel.

The Last of the Wine, The King Must Die, The Bull From the Sea, The Mask of Apollo, Fire From Heaven, and The Persian Boy were all best-sellers, and all depict life as it was in Greece up to the time of the fall of ancient Athens. In all her books, she showed great courage in exposing the truth as she saw it in politics and sexuality. She gave homosexuals a place in history.

In her private life, Renault fought strenuously against apartheid, censorship, and many forms of restriction and discrimination. Her greatest achievement was that through her books and public statements she guided thousands to seek out truth in themselves and in their environments. Mary Renault died in 1983.

Tribute must be paid to Mary Renault for remarkable literary talents. Her prose, at its best, is dazzling, her perceptions sharp and original, her dialogue natural to the ear. Of all the novels I have read on this theme [male homosexuality], it is the one that carries the most conviction, that seems to make the right distinctions, that shows the finest and the subtlest insight.

—SATURDAY REVIEW

Larry Kramer

ACTIVIST AND WRITER

Eventually I not only came to terms with being a gay man, but I came to recognize that I love being one, and want to be no other. That's been, and continues to be, a miraculously wonderful coming of age.

No one doesn't have an opinion about Larry Kramer. For some people, he is the grand Cassandra of AIDS and gay life, always right but never heeded—the voice crying in the wilderness, rousing the masses to fight. For others, he is less prophet than drama queen, his screeds melodramatic, with a talent for shooting himself—and his movement—in the foot. But whether Kramer rouses you or riles, he is without a doubt the fiercest, and perhaps most necessary, voice in the era he insists we call "the plague, the plague, the plague!"

Kramer's notoriety began long before AIDS reared its ugly head. It was *Faggots*, Kramer's 1978 satire of gay New York, that first forced people either to love or hate Larry Kramer. Some readers thought he had written a piercingly funny lampoon of sex, ambition and 1970s fast-lane sexual shenanigans—satirizing those gay men who shrugged off love in favor of fresh sensations. Others thought Kramer was cruel, unfair, his stiletto wit a weapon that revealed his own self-hatred and his envy of the lives of those he fictionalized.

Then came AIDS. Enduring fearful contempt from most gay people in 1981, Kramer and a few brave others founded Gay Men's Health Crisis, only to become almost instantly at odds over whether the group's first priority should be education and service or furious lobbying and anger. That tension continues to exist today in GMHC and in nearly all AIDS organizations. Kramer was cast aside by the organization that is still his first love. He wrote a play about the experience, *The Normal Heart*, which, as the dimension of the plague grew clear, defined both his reputation and the different attitudes of people confronting AIDS.

Struggling himself with HIV infection, Larry Kramer has never lost his single-minded focus, no matter how loud he yells. The author of the book of essays *Reports from the holocaust* (note the small "h") and the epic autobiographical drama *The Destiny of Me*, Kramer continues as a sort of freelance Jeremiah, raging at everyone from Bill Clinton to the *New York Times* to GMHC and ACT UP, his own babies—even as he works on his ever-growing epic novel of the plague, the plague, the plague. Angry, but never quite hopeless, Larry Kramer keeps *living*.

To read the full magnificent diatribe of Larry Kramer's writings about AIDS is to realize how necessary he is—like a blood transfusion. He does so much more than stand witness. His white hot rage and eloquent passion defy the complacency and hypocrisy of his and our enemies. How proud he makes me to be gay.

—Paul Monette
AUTHOR

Janis Ian

SINGER/SONGWRITER

I believe there is justice, I believe there is truth. Nothing in life is free; there is a price we have to pay for everything. The question then becomes—are you willing to pay the price? In my case, I was raised to be a Maccabee. It is not a matter of courage, but of conscience.

Less than a year after she announced to the world that she is a lesbian, Janis Ian stood near the edge of a stage at the annual Lesbian and Gay Pride rally in New York City and addressed the enormous crowd. Some of the people there were too young to remember the big hits that had established her; some had probably never heard of her. But when she spoke, with heartfelt joy, of her decision to come out of the closet, a warm glow spread through the audience, uniting them as one. Ian has been a professional since her teenage years and has had a great deal of performing experience, once being called "the best young singer in America" by none other than Ella Fitzgerald, but this moment filled her with a unique sense of accomplishment.

Always somewhat non-traditional in her approach to songwriting, Ian broke new ground on the radio airwaves in 1966 with *Society's Child,* a poignant ballad about a teenage interracial love affair. Then in 1975 she scored with *At Seventeen,* a song about being an ugly-duckling outcast in a world where appearance is everything. Many people who felt themselves to be outsiders in one way or another drew strength from the intelligence and poetry of her work.

And now, coming out as a lesbian in the conservative community of Nashville's musicians and songwriters, she has again achieved a major success. Rarely has anyone connected to the Nashville mainstream dared to acknowledge a lifestyle different from the norm. But the respect she commands from her peers and the love she receives from her fans have helped smooth her path. Now she is out, loud and proud; her career stronger than ever.

Not one to shy away from the hidden truths and harsh realities in her songs and in her life, Janis Ian has been a long-time inspiration to people everywhere.

Janis Ian speaks with an unusual, almost unnerving directness, as if honesty is no big deal—and that makes it easy to miss the bravery of what she is doing.

—Dudley Saunders
THE ADVOCATE

Photographed by James D. Wilson

Randy Shilts

JOURNALIST

AIDS is character-building. It's made me see all of the shallow things we cling to, like ego and vanity. Of course, I'd rather have a few more T-cells and a little less character.

A writer writes. Randy Shilts used his gifts to chronicle a generation of gay and lesbian life, and an epidemic which would change the community forever. When his voice was silenced by AIDS on February 17, 1994, the Mayor of San Francisco ordered the flags on all city buildings lowered to half mast. "I was the first token gay reporter in the country," said Shilts in an interview about his 1981 hiring by the *San Francisco Chronicle* to cover the gay community. "I didn't feel that bad about it, because there needed to be the first one."

Weeks before Shilts was hired, the *Chronicle* had printed an obscure announcement from the Centers for Disease Control, mentioning a mysterious outbreak of pneumonia and skin cancer among gay men. Three years later the disease had a name. In a December 1984 article, Shilts wrote, "The future that the doctors had predicted, with its staggering AIDS caseloads and widespread death, has arrived." At that time, the annual number of new cases in San Francisco had jumped from three hundred sixty-seven, to eight hundred thirty-three. Ten years later, the unimaginable annual number of new cases in that city alone would hover at something approaching thirty-three hundred. Shilts was among the first journalists to put a face on the nameless statistics of AIDS. In a series of profiles detailing the lives of individuals lost to the disease, he tried to communicate the impact of every life lost. "Each dying human being was part of a web of relationships," he wrote. "Each death touched mothers, fathers, lovers, friends, and neighbors."

In March 1987, on the same day he finished *And The Band Played On,* his best-seller that helped frame the national debate on AIDS, Shilts learned he was HIV-positive. He kept writing. In August 1992, the day before he would turn forty-one, he came down with pneumonia. From his hospital bed, he dictated the final pages of *Conduct Unbecoming,* his groundbreaking examination of gays and lesbians in the military. Two weeks before he died, he was interviewed by *60 Minutes.* "I never thought it was inevitable," he said about having AIDS. "And I can't say I'm bitter. You go through your 'why me?' stage, and it's very frustrating. Here I am at the pinnacle of my career. I could do anything in the world of journalism. And I'm left with a strange feeling that my life is somehow finished without being completed."

A writer lives by his words. In 1984 Shilts wrote about a man who had died of AIDS, "Like a stone dropped into a pool, his death sent ripples through the gay village, the straight city, and the country beyond it, and nobody who had known him would ever be quite the same again." A writer lives.

The entire world community has reason to honor Randy Shilts.

—William German
SAN FRANCISCO
CHRONICLE

Dr. Marjorie J. Hill

PUBLIC HEALTH OFFICIAL

When I first came out, I was this excited young lesbian and I was going to change the world. I used to fantasize that when I woke up tomorrow, the President would be a Black lesbian, the executives of IBM and the other corporations would be Black lesbians. Fifty percent, no, at least seventy-five percent of the U.S. Congress would be Black lesbians. That would make the world a better place.

If Dr. Marjorie J. Hill's youthful fantasy were to come true, it would certainly shift the balance of power in the world, but she has come to believe that it would not necessarily improve things. Her fifteen years of activism and public health advocacy have made her question the idea of a world where one group controls the wealth, makes the decisions, and determines what is valued. Her vision is of a place where differences are respected and everyone truly has equal opportunity. "In that world," Hill says, "it doesn't mean that the President always has to be a Black lesbian, but that sometimes it will happen."

As director of the New York City Mayor's Office for the Lesbian and Gay Community, Hill worked on the ill-fated "Children of the Rainbow" curriculum campaign which taught the value of every child's family structure. Hill believed that multiculturalism could get the attention of uninterested students by being relevant to their life experience. To her that meant including *Heather Has Two Mommies* in the curriculum. "The gay and lesbian family issue was a lightning rod to attack multiculturalism in education," she says. "It supposedly took away from the Three R's. But that isn't true. Children can read about Fannie Lou Hamer and write essays about Malcolm X. It's still arithmetic when the word problem starts out 'Adam and Steve are lovers and they buy a fifty-thousand-dollar home with ten percent down."

Hill also spearheaded the city's efforts to open the St. Patrick's Day Parade to the Irish Lesbian and Gay Organization, and marched with Mayor David N. Dinkins. During the parade, people threw things at Dinkins, shouted curses, and spat at him. "Dinkins was struck by the intensity of the bigotry and hatred expressed," she says. "The experience reminded him of the sixties in Selma, Alabama."

Currently, Hill is assistant vice president for special populations at the New York City Health and Hospitals Corporation, the nation's largest public health network. Much of her activism today comes down to one thing: "Racism and sexism have done more damage to the gay and lesbian civil rights movement than even the far right has. We will not win our rights until we learn the lessons of inclusion. We all have power and privilege of different kinds and to different degrees. Each of us must examine our power and privilege and be willing to share it with others."

In the gorgeous mosaic of New York City, Marjorie has made a definite contribution to the tile of social change.

—David N. Dinkins
NEW YORK CITY MAYOR

240

The Reverend Peter J. Gomes

MINISTER

It has not been my mission in life to make it easy for people to apply their labels to me. The only identity I own to the exclusion of all others is that of a child of God, created in the Maker's image. Everything else that I am or do comes from that, and I am unwilling to have the complexity of my human identity reduced merely to matters of race, sexuality, or political persuasion. I am so much more than that, and so are we all.

A pink triangle shattering into bits, pink shards flying off the page towards the reader—the cover illustration of the Fall 1991 *Peninsula* magazine, a conservative student publication at Harvard University—instantly gave students the gist of *Peninsula's* position on homosexuality. Yet it was the editors' reliance on the Bible to make many of their arguments that moved the Reverend Peter Gomes, the fiery minister of Harvard's Memorial Church and Plummer of Christian Values, to come out. "I felt that if I didn't speak out," says Gomes, "my integrity and capacity to speak out on anything after that would have been compromised."

By announcing that he is a "Christian who happens to be gay," Gomes gained a whole new sphere of influence. At first the press came to him to discuss the controversy at Harvard. It didn't take long though for Gomes to make the transition from news story to news source. The media began to seek him out for authoritative positions on everything from the relationship between Christianity and homosexuality to the search for the "gay gene," which he eventually ended up discussing with Ted Koppel on *Nightline*.

Gomes' experience of coming out prompted him to write a book, *Fighting for the Bible*, which included chapters on women, African-Americans, and lesbians and gays. Gomes' book proposal touched off a bidding war among publishers that made him one of America's highest paid openly gay authors. In explaining Gomes' extraordinary book contract with Morrow-Avon, the *New York Observer* described him as a "marketer's dream," and indeed, he is a true original who transcends obvious labels by reconciling so many of them: Not only is he a gay Christian, but also an African-American and a die-hard Republican—and, of course, a tenured Harvard professor as well.

With *Fighting for the Bible*, Gomes may become what many in the lesbian and gay community lament having only a handful of: a leader. If anyone has the oratorical skills to do so, it is Gomes. Martin Peretz, publisher of *The New Republic*, described Gomes' voice as "blessed by God." Gomes gave sermons at both Reagan's and Bush's inaugurations, and in 1979 *Time Magazine* chose him as one of the "star" preachers in the United States.

Peter Gomes is for me a model of how ministry to a university ought to be done. While too many other once great university chapels are empty, Gomes eloquently preaches to an appreciative full house.

—William H. Willimon
DUKE UNIVERSITY

242

Martina Navratilova

ATHLETE

Being a lesbian is not an accomplishment. I did not spend over thirty years of my life working my ass off, and trying to become the very best, so that I could be called 'Martina, the lesbian tennis player.' Labels are for filing. Labels are for clothing. Labels are not for people. Being homosexual, heterosexual, or bisexual, is not good or bad. It just is.

When was the last time anyone referred to "Joe Montana, the heterosexual football player"? That's a question Martina Navratilova thinks about a lot. She would like to see a world where everyone can come out, but also where the whole issue is beside the point. "Our goal is not to receive compassion, acceptance, or worse yet, tolerance," she says. "These imply that we are inferior. I don't want pity. Do you? But we have to be visible, so that we can be seen as intelligent, giving, and loving people with moral strength, dignity, and character. Once we are out, people will realize, 'You have the same problems. You have the same fashions. My God, you're just like us!' "

Navratilova has gone from being a tennis player focused only on her sport to becoming an outspoken advocate of lesbian and gay rights. She made headlines when she pointed out the double standard implicit in the outpouring of media affection for Magic Johnson upon his acknowledgment of being HIV-positive. What if it had been a woman, she wondered, or a gay man who had been having unprotected sex with multiple partners? Would he or she be championed as a hero? As a resident of Colorado, Navratilova has also been passionate in her activism against that state's Proposition 2, that would prohibit legal protection of lesbians and gay men.

Since defecting from Czechoslovakia in 1975, Navratilova's tennis triumphs have been unprecedented—as have public reports of her personal life. No other gay or lesbian athlete has ever been subjected to so much scrutiny, and her relationships have become fodder for the tabloid press. But through it all, Navratilova keeps a sense of humor. When asked what she wanted other Americans to know about her as a human being, she quipped, "What else would they want to know that they don't already know?"

Martina Navratilova is an inspiration to us all as she has championed athletics, human rights, and environmental causes in her road to stardom. She is the embodiment of a 'complete athlete,' in touch with her emotional, mental, physical, and spiritual well-being. Her ability to be strong on both the inside and the outside, has allowed her to continue her victorious career over a span of twenty-one years. I am certain that she will be at the forefront of many imperative issues affecting our society in the years to come.

—Billie Jean King
TENNIS CHAMPION

Paul Monette

AUTHOR AND POET

It's not enough to be an artist. If you live in cataclysmic times, if the lightning rod of history hits you, then all art is political, and all art that is not consciously so still partakes of the politics, if only to run away.

Paul Monette was a modestly successful novelist and screenwriter for roughly twelve years before he wrote his two autobiographical masterpieces, *Borrowed Time: An AIDS Memoir* in 1988, and the 1992 National Book Award-winner for non-fiction, *Becoming a Man: Half a Life Story.* In these intensely personal works, he broke the politics of silence about AIDS, homophobia, and homosexual love. At the same time, his memoirs reached far beyond gay readers; everyone identified with Monette's humanity. In describing his desperate attempt to run away from who he was, a gay man, he revealed the self-destruction created when one tries to conform to the majority.

The process of writing *Becoming a Man* was different from any book Monette had ever written. "During the first one hundred pages I loved writing it," he says. "Writing about my childhood was so releasing, freeing. I thought everyone should do it. But my enthusiasm began to curdle when I got to adolescence, and the rest of the book was very difficult. What happened was that when I was writing about being eighteen, I became eighteen: confused, depressed. It was the same with being twenty. I was reliving the pain of my earlier life. I was very glad to finish the book and I have no sense of incompleteness about it."

In addition to the National Book Award, Monette has earned three Lambda Literary Awards, the Don Kilhefner Founders Award, the PEN Center West Freedom to Write Award, the Medec 1990 Prix de Humanisme Medical, and several honorary doctorates. He claims Joan Didion and Flannery O'Connor as important influences because he says, "What they share is this almost breathtaking willingness to say who they are. Books are a repository for the truth—a balance against the unbelievable lies that politicians and the media tell us."

With all of Monette's literary achievement and scholarship, he wears his mantle lightly. He delights in new knowledge as a child, full of curiosity and wonder. Despite his rage at the hypocrisy and indifference of the church and the government towards AIDS, Monette possesses a playful, buoyant spirit that heals those around him. His friends know him as a brilliant storyteller who holds listeners spellbound with tales about his rich and wisely—observed life. He lives his life as he writes—openly, generously and passionately. Despite having lost two lovers to AIDS—Roger Horwitz, the subject of *Borrowed Time,* and Stephen Kolzak—and being diagnosed with AIDS in December 1991, he lives fully, sharing a loving and still joyous life with Winston Wilde high in the Hollywood Hills.

Paul Monette is one of the most courageous gay men who has ever lived.

—Larry Kramer
WRITER AND ACTIVIST

Dean LaBate

COMMUNITY HEALTH DIRECTOR

My own HIV test results and the loss of a lover and a host of friends made me even more determined to work for improved health care for the lesbian and gay AIDS communities.

Eight years ago, while working at a community clinic on Manhattan's Upper West Side, Dean LaBate tested HIV-positive. He had been on staff at the clinic for a number of years and had helped make sure it was gay and lesbian-inclusive, but he still felt much more needed to be done. "It's no secret," he says, "that lesbians and gay men have been underserved in health care." His work to broaden the health care provided to the gay community led him to his present position as executive director of the Community Health Project, New York's only lesbian and gay clinic. "Our mission is to provide quality health care for those who are HIV-infected," he says, "but also to be a place where lesbians, gay men, bisexuals and youth can walk in for any health concerns or preventative care and get the help they need."

As a child in New Jersey, LaBate knew what it was to be needy. "My father died when I was three," he says, "and raising two kids on a parochial school teacher's salary was never easy for my mother. I got a job in high school and kept it for eight years." He moved to Manhattan as a VISTA worker and organized a classroom program for special education children. Later, working at a community center, he would persuade teenagers, many of them gang members, to leave the street for a settlement house.

LaBate's career has been spent helping the disadvantaged and working for the public good, but joining the Community Health Project in 1992 was a serious challenge. He had to repair and strengthen health programs hampered by inadequate space and funding. In 1993 he hit on the ideal platform for advocating more government funding, and helped form the National Alliance of Lesbian and Gay Health Clinics which encompasses twelve facilities from coast to coast. "Our goal is to strengthen the collective voice of lesbian and gay health care, as well as HIV and AIDS health care in the national arena," he says. "We want our share of existing government dollars."

Living in Manhattan with his partner, Roderick Shade, LaBate has every reason to feel satisfied. He points to significant progress in funding at CHP, real headway in making a move to larger quarters, and increases in services, providing not only primary care and HIV assessment, but peer counseling and more inclusive health services tailored for lesbians and teenagers as well. "We take care of those who have the least access to health care," he says. "And I'm very proud of that."

Dean LaBate combines the administrative strength and progressive vision needed to ensure a strong future for this exemplary facility, the Community Health Project.

—Dr. Nicholas Rango
NEW YORK STATE
AIDS INSTITUTE

Photographed by Donal Holway
Courtesy Holway

Written by Denis Chicola

Rob Epstein and Jeffrey Friedman

FILMMAKERS AND LIFE-PARTNERS

Rituals do have power. It's very powerful to have a ritual where a community of people acknowledge and celebrate a relationship. —Jeffrey Friedman

We had a rabbi perform our wedding. She wore a sleeveless red mini-dress. My Aunt Sadie was much more freaked out about that, than about the fact that we were getting married. —Rob Epstein

In a matter of hours, Rob Epstein and Jeffrey Friedman, Oscar nominees and life partners, will leave the Four Seasons Hotel for the 1990 Academy Awards. *Common Threads: Stories From The Quilt,* the film they produced with Bill Couturie, is nominated for Best Documentary Feature. They spend their final moments before the ceremony practicing acceptance speeches while trying not to think about winning or losing. That day, their friend Christy Keith (a hairdresser and a lesbian) surprised them by driving to Los Angeles from San Francisco to make sure they were well-groomed for the evening—just in case. After all, a *billion* people watch the Oscars.

As the two men rehearsed in one room of the suite, Keith listened to them from the other room, where she was helping Epstein's sister with her hair. Trying out a few lines, Epstein thanked "all those fighting AIDS, especially the gay community." "Say 'lesbian,' " Christy shouted from the bathroom. Just hours later, as he stepped to the podium to accept the Academy Award for Best Documentary Feature, the whole world heard him thank "all those fighting AIDS, especially the gay *and lesbian* community."

That was Rob Epstein's second Oscar and Jeffrey Friedman's first. Epstein won *his* first in 1985 for *The Times of Harvey Milk,* the first film about a gay subject to win an Academy Award. Yet neither event qualifies as their proudest moment. "It was our wedding," they say. "Having gone through so many rituals around death," says Epstein, 'we felt that we also needed to have some *life* rituals. So Jeff and I had a wedding. It was wonderful. And it surprised me how much it meant to our family. It said to them we're in this for the long haul." "But we did it for us," Friedman emphasizes. "That's the reason to do it. It's not political. *But*—gay people should have every right to do it."

Epstein and Friedman met while working on a production for PBS. They became life partners, and then business partners when they formed the company, Telling Pictures, to make *Common Threads.* "It works for us," says Epstein. "The process is much more enjoyable for me having Jeffrey as a partner, to go through the difficult parts and the celebratory parts with him by my side. We're very lucky. There's no formula. There's no reason. It just has to do with the chemistry of who we are—together."

Rob and Jeffrey are gifted filmmakers who care passionately about their work. Their vision permeates Common Threads, *which speaks eloquently for their talent.*

—Cis Wilson
HBO

251

Harry Hay

GAY RIGHTS PIONEER
Above All, Audacity.

Back in 1950, in the teeth of total legal and social oppression, when Harry Hay first began to organize homosexuals, audacity was a queer survival skill. Hay also had ample supplies of determination. Activist, theorist, and visionary, he is gay history in the flesh. In his youth, working as a stage actor and screen extra, Hay acknowledges "sleeping his way" through 1930s Hollywood. An affair with actor Will Geer (later Grandpa Walton) introduced Hay to radical politics, labor organizing, and membership in the American Communist Party. By 1948, Hay conceived Bachelors Anonymous, a political organization for "androgynes."

Two years later, Hay and his lover Rudi Gernreich (eventually famous as the designer of the topless swimsuit) launched a series of secret meetings to promote Hay's vision of "an ethical homosexual culture." The Mattachine Society, guided by Hay's radical training and stage-honed charisma, became America's first viable gay organization, leading into the Stonewall era. Though his "Communist taint" meant Hay could not last in Mattachine's leadership, he stayed with the gay movement, and at the midpoint of his activist life co-founded the Los Angeles Gay Liberation Front in 1969. During the seventies, Hay and John Burnside, his life partner, moved to an Indian reservation in New Mexico where he continues his studies and writings about gay roles in other cultures and times.

Known from gay documentary films and the biography *The Trouble With Harry Hay,* he has become a feisty folk hero. The queer generation in particular find many of his still-radical views refreshing. His idea, for example, that gay people differ more from straights because of their consciousness than because of what they do in bed, became a foundation of the Radical Faerie movement, Hay's second wind in calling forth a new gay identity. Now at age eighty-two, he wears his trademark necklace, "a simple strand of false pearls, " precisely because he likes to see the reactions on the faces of nuclear families. Hay also seems to delight in upsetting establishment gays and lesbians. Invited to join the ultra-visible opening contingent at the 1993 March on Washington, Hay declined. "They were looking for a dinosaur," he said. "And besides, I wanted to march with my Faeries."

Harry Hay is the first person who said that gays are an oppressed minority. This was the heart and soul of the Mattachine movement, and all subsequent gay movements.

—Chuck Rowland
MATTACHINE SOCIETY
CO-FOUNDER

252

Written by Michael Feingold

John Corigliano and William M. Hoffman

COMPOSER AND PLAYWRIGHT

Our work is about love and how love can transcend even death—that's one of the grand themes of art.

It's December 1991, and the Metropolitan Opera is giving the world premiere of *The Ghosts of Versailles,* the first new American work it has commissioned and performed in twenty-five years. It is an opera for the '90s, a wild mixture of tunes, tone-rows, and chance-pitched electronic sounds, with a madcap deconstructed story in which ghosts and their fictional creations conspire to rewrite history—an opera that is an outrageous joke on opera, as well as a celebration of it. ("I couldn't follow the second act of *The Marriage of Figaro,*" says one character, "and this is even worse!")

Such an opera could only have been written by two gay men. It's no surprise that its two young-looking creators, wearing expressions of abashed solemnity while they take bravo after bravo, and while they listen, later, to artistic director James Levine telling them that their opera is the greatest achievement of his whole time at the Met, have come to this peak still trailing the afterglow of works that are landmarks of gay culture, artistic creations that make political statements by existing rather than by preaching.

Hoffman's *As Is,* one of the first notable plays about AIDS, has been done at innumerable theatres around the country since its successful Broadway run. Neither anonymous statistics nor passive victims, its heroes are gay lovers who learn during the course of the play that to rejoice in their love is to fight the plague: In the final scene, as an antidote to despair, they make love in a hospital bed.

The other side of the gay coin is Corigliano's *Symphony No. 1,* which had a tumultuous premiere in Chicago a few months before the unveiling of *The Ghosts of Versailles.* It is a vast, ferociously tragic eulogy, subtitled *Of Rage and Remembrance.* Its third movement, inspired by the AIDS Quilt, weaves together many short themes, settings by Corigliano of epitaph-like poems by Hoffman, in tribute to the endless list of friends they have lost to the epidemic. A choral version of it has been sung by gay men's choruses and vocal groups all over America.

How do Corigliano and Hoffman feel about their dual status as artists and gay role models? Mostly, they don't let it bother them. (When interviewed for this book, they claimed to be more interested in sex than in either art or politics.) Both are busy with a multitude of projects, Corigliano completing a guitar concerto, Hoffman putting the final touches on a contemporary love story. And together they're preparing the opening anthem for the next Gay Games. Creating in the mainstream, yet never ignoring their gay identity, they're a working model of the way artists who refuse to be marginalized can transform our culture.

Opera history was made at the premiere of The Ghosts of Versailles. *With the help of Hoffman's wise, witty libretto, Corigliano achieves moments as moving as any in Puccini, but with a spirituality that's more exalted.*

—David Patrick Stearns

USA TODAY

254

Photographed by Buck Ennis
Courtesy Strub

Sean O'Brien Strub

DIRECT-MAIL PIONEER

We gay people have not been very good at transferring accumulated wealth from one generation to another. It's especially important in our community to develop strong institutions and to pass along our skills to our young people.

As a Georgetown University student, Sean Strub met Alan Baron, publisher of *The Baron Report*, an influential Washington newsletter. Baron had written a fundraising letter for the newly organized Human Rights Campaign Fund and was looking for a famous homosexual who would be willing to sign it. Strub had met Tennessee Williams and thought Williams might let them use his name. "I had my *spiel* all prepared," Strub says. "He read the letter and asked a couple of questions about it. He thought the letter was fine, and I said, 'Well, your signature on it would raise so much money for this group, at least $200,000.' He said, 'Baby, *my* signature is worth at least $200,000 on this letter? Well, why don't you just give me a check?' Then we talked about everything else in the world, and I thought he wasn't going to sign it. I was starting to make the first moves to go, and he said, 'What about your letter? Don't you want me to sign your letter?' And I said, 'Sure.' I was so excited, I started to cry, and he couldn't understand why."

Growing up in Iowa City, Strub recalls how his $5 membership in the American Civil Liberties Union, with its newsletters and invitations, was a means of communication that went far beyond anything he could learn in his immediate family environment. It was that sense of participation that made him think he might be successful with Tennessee Williams. It was also what started him on a path to becoming a direct-mail fundraising consultant to gay and lesbian rights and AIDS organizations, bringing that same sense of participation to thousands of gay men and lesbians, while providing a solid base of financial support for the movement. His businesses have raised over $20 million for gay and lesbian groups, while organizations he has trained have gone on to raise many times that amount on their own.

Strub is the author of *Rating America's Corporate Conscience*, and—with Daniel B. Baker—of *Cracking the Corporate Closet*. Both books survey how large companies relate to society at large, and to their gay and lesbian employees and customers. He has also recently founded *POZ*, a new magazine focusing on topics related to being HIV-positive. He is proudest, though, of how his own business, Strubco, trains dozens of committed young activists in the fundraising and marketing techniques he developed.

Sean really pioneered direct-mail fundraising for gay and AIDS organizations. A lot of the reason was because he was so entrepreneurial, and willing to do all this work.

—Ken Dawson
SENIOR ACTION
IN A GAY ENVIRONMENT

Ned Rorem

COMPOSER AND WRITER

You do grow weary of 'courageous' announcements of Homosexual Studies—of scientists achieving breakthroughs on this 'complex condition.' Do the scientists have courses in Heterosexual Studies? Might they then conclude that homosexuality is in fact a simple condition? That problem solved, they could go on to something important, like a cure for asthma. —from An Absolute Gift

In the late sixties there were no homosexuals in America. Not if you watched the news, read the newspapers, listened to talk shows or read people's memoirs. Certain figures were "known" to be homosexual; that is, however, only if you were already "in the know." If you were looking for real life figures—not characters in novels or in poems—there appeared to be few, if any, prominent Americans willing to state unequivocally in print that they themselves were homosexual. Virgil Thompson did not. Paul Bowles did not. Leonard Bernstein did not. Aaron Copeland did not. Gertrude Stein did not. Gore Vidal was "bi-sexual." Tennessee Williams "covered the waterfront," whatever that meant.

Ned Rorem was a homosexual. He said so in his published diaries kept over his many years in Paris, Morocco, and New York. These books were filled with provocative observations about music, art, civilization (and its lack). Throughout, one encountered the titles of innumerable literary jewels, but most vividly, one met Ned Rorem, whose bold conceit it was to kiss and tell between concerts, meals, and so many theoretical postulates. Here was an articulate, complicated, and altogether self-possessed American who wrote music, had interesting and talented friends, a loving mother and father—a man who made a living and traveled the world, *and slept with other men.* And with some frequency. And with little or no apparent torment. In fact, Rorem insisted over and over again that homosexuality was in and of itself neither interesting nor important. It was as defining, in his estimation, as having brown hair or green eyes. It was a context, rather than content. What kind of person or artist you were would depend upon the quality of your efforts—your vision, your clarity, your craft. The fact of one's gayness was an element with no inherent negative or positive value. This was as refreshing to hear back then as it is now.

Whatever motivated Rorem to set this notion forward in that hysterical and repressive age, one can only guess. Call it bravery or foolhardiness or naked self-promotion, to those coming of age in the sixties it was nothing short of remarkable. Add to that the bounty of lovely, unfashionably tonal music Rorem has contributed year after year, and one has as unlikely a gay hero as one could ever wish for. That's certainly the best kind.

Rorem can take a poem and transform it into sound with absolute inevitability. He understands the secrets of the art song, knows that all music stems from sung expression, and instinctively finds the precise phrase and cadence that lie hidden in the written word.

—John Gruen
CRITIC AND BIOGRAPHER

Vivienne Armstrong and Louise Young

TEXAS DEMOCRATS

We were thrilled to ride in President Clinton's inaugural parade. When the gays and lesbians along Pennsylvania Avenue saw us coming, they would point and shout, 'There they are!' When we raised our clasped hands, the couples in the crowd raised their hands. We waved our rainbow flags and they waved theirs back. Some gave us a thumbs up. In sign language, others signed us, 'I love you.'

Vivienne Armstrong and Louise Young found it hard to believe—there they were, representing gay and lesbian families on the "Family of America" float in Washington. D.C., riding along with single-parent, multi-racial, old, young and traditional families. The couple felt included in a way they had never felt before. "This was history in the making," they say. "For the first time open gays and lesbians had been included in the inaugural parade."

It had been a long journey to that parade route. The couple first met during a Gay Liberation Front meeting at the University of Colorado in 1971. "It was a classic meeting," says Young. "Girl meets girl across a crowded room, love at first sight and all that," and they have been together ever since. When Travis County, the Texas county which includes Austin, passed the first domestic partnership law in the state, they were among the first to register. "We'll fly to Hawaii and get married," says Armstrong, "as soon as Hawaii gets its act together and makes it legal."

Moving to Dallas in the mid 1970s, the couple has successfully combined Young's software engineering responsibilities at Texas Instruments and Armstrong's community nursing career, and a shared passion for social activism with their out-of-the-closet relationship. Young was the first woman president of the Dallas Gay and Lesbian Alliance and the first openly gay or lesbian person elected to the Texas State Democratic Party Executive Committee. Armstrong, a recipient of the American Nurses Association's Search for Excellence Award, became the founding co-chair of the Lesbian/Gay Political Coalition of Dallas, and has been a Democratic Party Precinct Chair since 1984.

Together, Armstrong and Young have spurred tremendous progress in the Texas Democratic Party. When they first moved to Dallas, there was a very small number of socially conscious, openly lesbian activists. Few Democratic Party leaders would even talk to them. But things had changed considerably by 1991, when the Democratic Party Executive Committee passed a resolution commemorating the couple's twentieth anniversary.

Vivienne and Louise are loyal and committed young women. They are a positive influence and an asset to this city, and have dedicated themselves to public service. They are making Dallas a better place for all of us.

—Annette Strauss
FORMER DALLAS MAYOR

CONTRIBUTORS

VAL PENN ADDAMS is a writer living in Los Angeles. He is currently working on his fifth screenplay, a children's book, and his one man performance piece, *The Nikita Khurschef Songbook.*

DOUG ALLEN is a writer and artist whose previous writings include *The Dreamaster* and *Look Through the Window.* A devout American who has yet to travel abroad, he makes his home in Los Angeles, New York City, and Massachusetts.

ED ANDERSON is producer and host of *Ed Anderson's Journal,* a cable television show dealing with political and social issues. He is a graduate of Stanford University and Stanford Law School and works as a lawyer and journalist in Los Angeles.

SAMUEL BERNSTEIN is a playwright and screenwriter living on both coasts. Plays include *Love Songs, Lavinia is for Lovers,* and *The Liquidation of Granny Peterman;* musicals: *Bobby, The Peddler,* and the upcoming *Magic Boys.* His film *Bloodlines* will go into production in early 1995.

TERRY BOGGIS is director of communications at New York's Lesbian and Gay Community Services Center. She is also a member of the steering committee of Center Kids, the Center's family project.

CHRIS BONEAU formed Boneau/Bryan-Brown with Adrian Bryan-Brown in 1991. Among their clients are *Angels in America, Tommy, Beauty and the Beast,* and *Sunset Boulevard,* among others. He serves on the board of BC/EFA and is an adjunct professor of Theatre Studies at Columbia.

NINA C. BROWN is a writer and political organizer. Born in New York City, and schooled in Los Angeles, she has found her niche in Wilmington, North Carolina, where she serves as director of programs for the local gay and lesbian center.

CHARLES BUSCH is the author of the plays *Vampire Lesbians of Sodom, Psycho Beach Party, The Lady in Question* and *Red Scare on Sunset.* His first novel *Whores of Lost Atlantis* was published by Hyperion in 1993. He lives in New York's West Village.

CHIQUI CARTEGENA is a freelance journalist who works and lives in New York City. Since 1990 she has been working on a video documentary about gays in the military that profiles the story of Sgt. Perry Watkins.

HOWARD CASNER is a playwright living in Chicago. His work has been seen in Chicago, Los Angeles, Seattle, and New York, and has been published by Dialogus Publishing. He is the Chicago correspondent for the *Purple Circuit.*

MARK CHESNUT's writing has appeared in *The Advocate, Emerge, Genre,* and *Ten Percent.* He is an editor at Resident Newspapers in New York City; editor-in-chief of *Skyjack Magazine;* and contributing producer for the PBS-TV program *In the Life.*

DENIS CHICOLA is an award-winning filmmaker based in Los Angeles. His work can be seen on PBS, MTV, and wherever commercials are aired. He is producing *You Hear Their Voices,* a documentary about a writing workshop for those affected by AIDS.

ADRIENE CORBIN is a screenwriter and freelance writer living in Los Angeles. An alumna of Columbia University School of Journalism in New York City, she began her career as a writer, and then editor, for various business magazines.

TEE CORINNE is a visual artist, editor and writer, whose works include *The Body of Love, Riding Desire, Intricate Passions,* and *The Poetry of Sex: Lesbians Write the Erotic.*

BOB DALLMEYER is a political activist and freelance writer living in Los Angeles. His short stories and articles appear monthly in *IDEAS* and the *Orange County Blade.* He has also published one book of poetry entitled *SNAPSHOTS.*

JANE DeLYNN's novels include *Don Juan in the Village, Real Estate, In Thrall* and *Some Do.* She wrote about the Gulf War for *Mirabella* and *Rolling Stone,* and has been published in numerous magazines and anthologies.

GEORGE DORRIS was born in Eugene, Oregon but lives and teaches in New York City. He writes on dance and music for *Ballet Review, The Dancing Times* and *Dance Chronicle,* which he co-edits with Jack Anderson.

MALKA DRUCKER is the co-author of *RESCUERS: Portraits of Moral Courage in the Holocaust* and the award-winning author of over fifteen children's books. An admirer of Paul Monette, she is grateful to call him a friend.

GEORGE DUREAU has shown his paintings, sculpture, and photography throughout the United States and Europe. He now lives and works in New Orleans.

STANLEY E. ELY is a language teacher and freelance writer living in New York. He is on the board of the Publishing Triangle and Community Health Project, and his work has appeared in *Genre, Texas Triangle,* and *Air Destinations.*

DAVID B. FEINBERG is the author of *Eighty-Sixed, Spontaneous Combustion,* and the forthcoming *Queer and Loathing.* He is a member of ACT UP/NY and lives in New York City.

MICHAEL FEINGOLD is a playwright, translator, and chief theater critic for *The Village Voice.* He recently edited *Grove New American Theater,* which includes significant gay-themed and anti-censorship plays by Ethyl Eichelberger, David Greenspan, Karen Finley, and Mac Wellman.

AYOFEMI FOLAYAN is a grandmother, wordsmith, and actorvist from Los Angeles. She teaches creative writing at the Gay and Lesbian Community Services Center and publishes essays and fiction in feminist, people of color, and gay and lesbian publications.

MARC GELLER is a San Francisco-based freelance photojournalist who has been documenting gay life for over a decade. His clients include national magazines and corporations, as well as community newspapers and organizations.

RICK GERHARTER is a San Francsico-based photojournalist who has documented the queer community for over eight years. His work has appeared in *Newsweek* and *The Economist,* as well as *The Leather Journal* and *Whorezine.*

SIMON GLICKMAN is a musician and freelance writer living in Los Angeles. His work has appeared in *Contemporary Musicians, Popular Music and Society,* and *Bricolage.* He is twenty-nine and has a PhD in English from Oxford.

TREY GRAHAM is a staff writer on *The Washington Blade.* His essay on JEB (Joan E. Biren) is adapted from a profile which originally ran in the *Blade.*

DAVID GROFF is a New York writer whose work has appeared in *American Poetry Review, Christopher Street, The Georgia Review, OW, Seven Days, Wigwag,* and *Men on Men 2: Best New Gay Fiction.* He is a senior editor at Crown Publishers.

MARK HAILE is a journalist with the Black gay and lesbian newsmagazine *BLK.* His work has been published widely in both the gay and non-gay press. Born in Africa in 1956, he now lives in Chinatown Heights overlooking Los Angeles.

JOHN HAMMOND is a staff writer with *New York Native.* He joined the gay movement in 1972 with Gay Activists Alliance and is a founder of Gay History Archives.

ALAN HELMS teaches American poetry at the University of Massachusetts in Boston. He has just completed a memoir titled *Damaged Goods.*

DONAL F. HOLWAY is a New York photographer. Once a *Times* staffer, he now specializes in subjects ranging from Presidents, to Barbie, to the Brooklyn Bridge and built his own panoramic camera. If the project is right, he will work for food or love.

SHARON P. HOLLAND is an assistant professor in the English department at Stanford. One of her forthcoming articles is *To Touch the Mother's C(o)untry: Siting Audre Lorde's Erotics* in *Lesbian Erotics: Practices and Critiques.*

DANIEL JACOBSON is a freelance writer living in New York. He has written on dance, music, and theatre for *The New York Native* and *Ballet Review.* His book reviews and translations from the French have appeared in the *Los Angeles Times.*

JEB (JOAN E. BIREN) is an internationally known photographer. Collections of her work include *Eye to Eye: Portraits of Lesbians, Making a Way: Lesbians Out Front, For Love and For Life,* and the documentary video *A Simple Matter of Justice.*

DAVID JEFFERSON writes about entertainment, pop culture, and gay issues for *The Wall Street Journal,* and is a member of the National Lesbian and Gay Journalists Association. A Los Angeles native, he lives with his lover Christopher Hartley and their two cats Darius and Norma.

ARNIE KANTROWITZ is an associate professor of English at the College of Staten Island, and was a founding member of GLAAD and vice-president of GAA/NY. He is the author of *Under the Rainbow: Growing Up Gay,* and is currently working on a biography of Walt Whitman.

TOM W. KELLY is a freelance writer and playwright who lives in San Francisco. Several of his critical essays were published in *Gay and Lesbian Literature,* his feature articles and reviews have appeared nationally, and his plays have run successfully in San Francisco, Los Angeles, and Seattle.

SUZE LANIER divides her time between New York and Los Angeles, photographing fashion assignments when she is not on location shooting film stars, recording artists, and best-selling authors.

ANNIE LEIBOVITZ is an internationally celebrated photographer whose work has appeared in numerous publications all over the world, including *Vanity Fair* and *Rolling Stone.*

STAN LEVENTHAL is the author of *Mountain Climbing in Sheridan Square, A Herd of Tiny Elephants, Faultlines, The Black Marble Pool, Candy Holidays,* and *Skydiving on Christopher Street.*

CRAIG LUCAS is the author of the plays, *Missing Persons, Reckless, Blue Window, Prelude to a Kiss,* and *God's Heart,* as well as screenplays for *Longtime Companion* and *Prelude to a Kiss.* He co-created *Marry Me a Little,* and has written the librettos for the operas, *Orpheus in Love* and *Breedlove.*

PATSY LYNCH is a freelance photo-journalist in the D.C. area. For fifteen years she has documented the lesbian and gay community, and works regularly for Associated Press (AP), *Time, Newsweek, Elle, People, Out, The Advocate,* and the *New York Times.*

ERIC MARCUS has written four books, including *The Male Couple's Guide, Making History, Expect the Worst (You Won't Be Disappointed),* and *Answers to 300 of the Most Frequently Asked Questions About Gays and Lesbians.* He is a graduate of Vassar College and Columbia University.

LAURA MARKOWITZ is a National Magazine Award-winning writer, and associate editor of *The Family Therapy Networker.* She has written for *Glamour, The Utne Reader, Lambda Book Report, Sojourner,* and other publications.

DAWN LUNDY MARTIN is a freelance writer currently finishing her Master's in Poetry at San Francsico State. She is an editorial assistant at *Feminist Bookstore News,* and her poems have been most recently published in *Transfer Magazine;* her non-fiction in *Forward Motion.*

LAWRENCE C. MASS, M.D. is the co-founder of Gay Men's Health Crisis and the author of *Dialogues of the Revolution, Volumes I and II.* His most recent book, *Confessions of a Jewish Wagnerite: Memoirs of Being Gay and Jewish in America,* will be published by Cassell.

BRUCE MIRKEN, a recently transplanted San Franciscan, has written for *Men's Health, Ten Percent, The Advocate, AIDS Treatment News,* the *San Francisco Bay Guardian* and the *Los Angeles Reader.*

DAVID MORGAN has been based in New York since 1975. He shoots portrait, commercial, fashion, and fine art. His spirited imagery *(White Party)* and sculptural studies of men with men *(Embrace),* have been published world-wide.

BENJAMIN MORRISON was born and lives in New Orleans. He has spent nearly two decades as a television critic for the *Times-Picayune* newspaper, allowing him to consort with Dietrich, Baryshnikov, and Fabio—though not all at once.

JULIE MULLARD, longtime companion of the author Mary Renault, is a retired registered nurse living in South Africa.

HILARY MULLINS' acclaimed first novel *The Cat Came Back* was nominated for a Lambda Literary Award. She lives in Oakland, California with her partner April Evans.

PAULA NEVES is a writer and editor for *Network Magazine.* She has contributed fiction and poetry to various gay and lesbian anthologies coming soon to a bookstore near you.

KAREN OCAMB is a former associate producer at CBS News, and has been a freelance writer, photographer, and independent producer since 1988. She has written for *Los Angeles Magazine,* the *Hollywood Reporter, California Magazine, The Advocate, Genre,* and the *Lesbian News.*

JUDI PARKS is a photojournalist in the San Francisco Bay area. In the year and a half since she resumed her photography career, she has had over one thousand publications of her photos. Also a writer, she is working on a photo and text project documenting aspects of homelessness in America.

ROBERT PATRICK's fifty published plays include the Glasgow Citizens' Theatre World Playwright Award-winning *Kennedy's Children* and *Untold Decades.* He received the International Thespian Founders Award in 1980 and his novel, *Temple Slave,* is available from Masquerade Books.

JILL POSENER is a photo journalist from London. She is the author of two photographic collections, *Spray It Loud* and *Louder Than Words.* Her work has appeared in the anthologies *Stolen Glances, Dagger,* and *Femalia,* as well as in the *Village Voice,* the *New York Times, Cosmopolitan,* and *Out.*

ELIZABETH RANDOLPH's work has appeared in *Colorlife Magazine, Cocodrilo, Contemporary Lesbian Writers Of The United States: A Bio-Bibliographical Critical Sourcebook* (Greenwood Publications), and a collection tentatively entitled *Great Lesbian Love Poetry* (St. Martin's Press, 1995)

DALE REYNOLDS has been a professional actor since 1968, and a journalist for the world's gay and lesbian press since 1986. His tour-guide, *L.A. Scene,* (GMP/1992) will be reprinted in early 1995, and he is moving into feature film production this year.

GABRIEL ROTELLO writes a weekly column on gay and lesbian issues for *New York Newsday.* In 1989 he co-founded *OutWeek,* and served as its editor in chief for two years. He has written for the *Village Voice, Out, New York Magazine,* and numerous other publications.

RICHARD ROUILARD is a senior editorial consultant at the *Los Angeles Times.* He was editor-in-chief of *The Advocate,* a senior editor at the *Los Angeles Herald Examiner,* and co-founder and editor of *L.A. Style Magazine.* He is a Pulitzer Prize-nominated reporter.

MARJORIE RUSHFORTH is a gay/lesbian/AIDS activist and was the first openly lesbian attorney in Orange County, California. Her legal victories include the 1987 federal case which, for purposes of legal protection, established AIDS as a handicap. She is now writing a biography of Ivy Bottini.

DOUG SADOWNICK is an award-winning journalist in Los Angeles. His first novel, *Sacred Lips of the Bronx,* has just been published by St. Martin's Press.

FRANCESCO SCAVULLO is an internationally celebrated photographer who has shot most of the famous people living in the twentieth century.

JOHN R. SELIG is a writer and photographer living in Dallas with his sixteen-year-old son Nathaniel, three cats, and a macaw. He has an MBA from the University of Chicago and extensive restaurant industry marketing experience.

JULE BROWN SIBLEY is the younger sister of Howard Brown. A native of Ohio, and graduate of Oberlin College, she is coordinator of human services for Mamaroneck Village/Westchester County.

BARBARA SMITH is a Black feminist writer and activist who has participated in the lesbian and gay movement since the mid-1970s. She is the editor of *Home Girls: A Black Feminist Anthology,* co-founder and publisher of *Kitchen Table: Women of Color Press,* and lives in Albany, New York.

GEOFFREY STAPLES is a freelance writer living in Dallas. He is founder and editor of *Strategic Systems Newsletter,* a publication for corporate chief information officers.

KAREN SUNDQUIST is managing editor of *The Family Therapy Networker,* and a freelance writer and editor in the Washington, D.C. area.

MICHAEL SZYMANSKI is a Los Angeles journalist for the *Los Angeles Times, Entertainment Weekly* and the *New York Times Syndicate,* as well as *Genre* and *The Advocate.* He is writing on bisexuality in Dr. Ruth Westheimer's *Encyclopedia of Sexuality.*

DAVID THORPE is an associate editor at *10 PERCENT* magazine. He is currently at work on an autobiographical novel entitled *My Generation X.*

STUART TIMMONS' writing on historical and cultural stories spans fifteen years. His 1990 biography, *The Trouble With Harry Hay,* was nominated for a Lambda Literary Award.

MICHAEL VAN DUZER is a graduate of U.S.C., and is a prize-winning playwright and director. He has written criticism for *L.A. Dispatch,* worked extensively for Broadway Cares/Equity Fights AIDS, and is a member of the Dramatists Guild.

ERIC K. WASHINGTON is a freelance writer who has contributed articles to *The Village Voice, Transition, Metropolis, Elle Decor,* and *Out* (in which this profile was originally published in a lengthier form). He is also the New York editor of *BLK,* the national newsmagazine that spotlights the African-American lesbian and gay community.

MARY WINGS is the author of the award-winning *She Came Too Late, She Came in a Flash* and 1993 Lambda Literary Award-nominee *Divine Victim.* She is a 1994-5 Raymond Chandler Fulbright nominee and her books have been translated into Dutch, German, Japanese, and Spanish.

ALBERT J. WINN is a nationally celebrated fine art photographer living in Santa Monica, California. He is the recent winner of a grant from the National Endowment of the Arts.

SARA WOLF is a freelance writer, mother, and managing editor of *High Performance* magazine. She lives in Los Angeles.

DAN WOOG is a freelance writer whose work appears in both the gay and mainstream press. His book on gay and lesbian issues in American schools will be published by Alyson Press in 1995. He lives in Westport, Connecticut.

JOELLE YUNA is a principal in Sky Ladder Communications, a three-year-old communications consultancy located in San Francisco. She and her associates work primarily with women-owned businesses, providing editorial services, marketing communications, photography, design, and production expertise to clients nationwide.

OTHER CONTRIBUTORS

JOAN ALDEN	SEAN GALLAND	JAMES LEVITT	JOHNNY ROZSA
GENE BAGNATO	KRISTI K. GASAWAY	TRACY LITT	SABRINA SOJOURNER
TRACY BAIM	ROBERT GIARD	BLAKE LITTLE	JAY THOMPSON
CRAWFORD BARTON	MORGAN GWENWALD	DAVID MARTIN	JEFFREY TITCOMB
TOM BIANCHI	DR. SCOTT HILL	ALAIN McLAUGHLIN	BECKY VILLASENDOR
DONNA BINDER	DOUG HINCKLE	ANN MEREDITH	JAMES D. WILSON
JOHN BODINGER	HONOWITZ	DAVID RAE MORRIS	BILL WOODFORD
BEVERLY BROWN	MARILYN HUMPHRIES	ELLEN NEIPRIS	IRENE YOUNG
PAUL CHINN	REGGIE IGE	DAN NICOLETTA	KEN ZANE
ANNE DOWIE	GLENN JESSEN	REGINALD PEARMAN	
BUCK ENNIS	ANNALISA KRAFT	RON REAGAN	
JEROME FRIAR	NICK LAMMERS	STACY ROSENSTOCK	

UNCOMMON ANGELS

KATHERINE ACEY	GAYLE GOULD	JED MATTES	JOHN R. SELIG
LINDA ALBEND	DON GRASSO	TIM MCFEELY	BRIAN SHAFFER
ALDO ALVAREZ	DAVID GROFF	DOUG MENDINI	BILL SHANAHAN
RON ANDEREGG	KEITH HALPERIN	ANITA MERK	YVONNE SHERMAN
EDWARD ANDERSON	RAYMOND HART	MARTIN MERLE	CLAYTON SHERMAN
LAURA AQUILAR	JEFF HENRY	PAUL MONETTE	GEOFFREY STAPLES
TRACY BAIM	STEPHEN E. HERBITS	DAVID MORGAN	SEAN STRUB
SEALE BALLINGER	GAYLORD HOFTIEZER	BRETT MORROW	MARK TADLOCK
GAY BLOCK	ANDREW HOLLERAN	ROBERT NAPOLITANO	DAVID TOSER
TERRY BOGGIS	DONAL HOLWAY	OTTO E. NELSON	TOWNHOUSE
JERRALD L. BOSWELL	RICK HYMAN	STACEY NELSON	JANICE THOM
KERMIT BROWN	JOHN HUTSON	PETER NEUFELD	SARA HORMEL
SEAN BYRNES	LEIGH HUTTICK	TONY NEUFEILD	VON QUILLFELD
DENIS CHICOLA	IMPACT VISUALS	KAREN OCAMB	MARC WANSHEL
CHRIS CHRISTIAENS	MICHAEL ISRAEL	JOHN O'CONNOR	ERIC WEIGLE AND
BARRY COLEMAN	MITCHELL IVERS	NADINE ONO	JAMES BERRY
BILL CWALENSKI	JASON JACOBS	STEPHAN OXENDINE	MARK WILLEMS
MELISSA DALE	MARVIN JARMELL	JUDI PARKS	KEN WILLIS AND
DENNIS DANIELS	JEB (JOAN E. BIREN)	PHILLIP PARKS	CHRIS DUNCAN
GYPSY DASILVA	SUSAN K. JESTER	ANDRÉ PASTORIA	ROBERT WOODWORTH
PETER DOLGIN	TODD JONES	JOHN PENNE	JERALD T. YOUNG
KEITH DUNHILL	MICHAEL JORDAN	JAMES PEPPER	
JASON DRAPKIN	MICHELLE KARLSBERG	JEFF PICA	
STANLEY ELY	MORRIS KIGHT	ROBERT PIERSON	
GAIL ENSINGER	RICHARD LABONTE	PAUL POUX	
DAVID FLETCHER	ANNIE LEIBOVITZ	DAVID PFINGSLTER	
FLYLEAF	PACO LOPEZ-BAEZ	LEN PRINCE	
TIMOTHY FOSTER	BILL LUCKEY	ROBERT RODRIEGUEZ	
STEPHEN R. FRANKEL	SANDRA LUCOT	DORIT ROSEN	
DR. LEN FRISHER	PATSY LYNCH	ERIC ROSEN	
RAYMOND GARCIA	JEANNE MANFORD	EDDI SARAFATY	
ARCH GARLAND	ROGER MAPES	FRANCESCO SCAVULLO	
STEVEN GOLD	ERIC MARCUS	MICHAEL SCHAEFER	
JIM GONZALES	PAUL MATTA	JACK SCHLEGEL	

INDEX